Communications
in Computer and Information Science 498

T0224385

Fernando Koch   Felipe Meneguzzi
Kiran Lakkaraju (Eds.)

Agent Technology for Intelligent Mobile Services and Smart Societies

Workshop on Collaborative Agents,
Research and Development, CARE 2014
and Workshop on Agents, Virtual Societies
and Analytics, AVSA 2014
Held as Part of AAMAS 2014
Paris, France, May 5-9, 2014
Revised Selected Papers

 Springer

Volume Editors

Fernando Koch
Samsung Research Institute
Campinas, SP, Brazil
E-mail: fkoch@acm.org

Felipe Meneguzzi
Pontifical Catholic University
of Rio Grande do Sul
Porto Alegre, RS, Brazil
E-mail: felipe.meneguzzi@pucrs.br

Kiran Lakkaraju
Sandia National Laboratories
Albuquerque, NM, USA
E-mail: klakkar@sandia.gov

ISSN 1865-0929
ISBN 978-3-662-46240-9
DOI 10.1007/978-3-662-46241-6
Springer Heidelberg New York Dordrecht London

e-ISSN 1865-0937
e-ISBN 978-3-662-46241-6

Library of Congress Control Number: 2015932150

Typesetting: Camera-ready by author, data conversion by Scientific Publishing Services, Chennai, India

Printed on acid-free paper

Springer is part of Springer Science+Business Media (www.springer.com)

Preface

This volume comprises the joint proceedings of two workshops that took place in conjunction with the 13th International Autonomous Agents and Multiagent Systems (AAMAS) Conference: the Collaborative Agents – Research and Development (CARE 2014)[1] workshop and the Agents, Virtual Societies and Analytics (AVSA 2014)[2] workshop. Both workshops are international workshops hosted in conjunction with the 13th International Conference on Autonomous Agents and Multiagent Systems (AAMAS 2014), in Paris, France. The common ground between the two exists in the intersection between a top-down experimental approach and a bottom-up interaction analysis. We present a cohesive discussion by selecting a handful of representative papers from the events. The main topics in these workshops were: computational social sciences, smart societies, social applications, urban intelligence, intelligent mobile services, mobile service environment, and context intelligence.

These workshops shared an interest in new models of communication and interaction. The research leads to innovative technologies that allow for intelligence application, collaborative services, and methods to better understand society, interactions, and problems.

The thematic focus of CARE 2014 was "CARE for Intelligent Mobile Service." The thematic developed around the dream of intelligent mobile services that assist people during their day-to-day activities in homes, offices, and healthcare facilities is compelling. Relevant questions for this workshop were: How can we create computational models, representations, algorithms and protocols to enable the next generation of intelligent mobile services? What are the new challenges when service computing becomes mobile? What new functionalities and effectiveness can make use of collaborative models in mobile services? The CARE 2014 workshop received 28 papers submitted through the workshop website, from which we selected nine papers for publication, all being republished as extended versions in this volume.

The AVSA workshop focused on virtual worlds – a rich, engaging domain through which humans can connect, fight, communicate, make social groups, and live, such as in the real world. The discussion revolved around the view of virtual worlds as a laboratory for the real world and alternative windows onto human interaction. The workshop selected six papers for publication, from which we selected one paper for this volume.

Submissions came from diverse countries in the Americas (Brazil, USA, Canada, others), Europe (The Netherlands, Spain, Germany, others), Australia, New Zealand, and others.

---

[1] http://www.care-workshops.org/care2014

[2] https://sites.google.com/site/aamasavsa2014

We selected ten papers as representative contributions for this volume. The selections are detailed below, highlighting their relation and contribution to the domain of knowledge in the scope of the workshop.

In the first paper, "Urbosenti: An Ubiquitous Service-Oriented Architecture for Urban Sensing," Rolim et al. propose a sensing architecture for urban environments. The platform provides the mechanisms for multi-modal data collection and the development of new sensors. The research aims to use humans as part of the sensor process in order to promote human–machine collaboration and supervised learning. The significance relates to technologies for collaborative services to support issues in urban intelligence and smart city scenarios.

In the second paper, "Geo-fencing-Based Disaster Management Service," Szczytowski focuses on enhanced communication in disaster scenarios. The challenges in the process of sharing social media information related to unstructured, unreliable, and dispersed data are described. The paper proposes an approach based on combining a geo-fencing technology with a social network platform to address the issue. The approach helps foster collaboration of agents that are both likely to be affected by a disaster, but also in the best position to deal with and collaborate on solving the local problem. Thus, geofences become a filter for the "noise" often associated with social network communication. The illustrative scenarios focus on disaster management and "virtual fences" focus on analyzing social behavior toward local problems.

This development is significant in supporting innovative technologies that allow for intelligence application and collaborative services. In addition to the contribution to intelligent recommendation systems, it promotes the creation of customized virtual worlds. This environment would be useful as a laboratory for the real disaster situation scenarios.

In the third paper, "Knowledge-Level Integration for JaCaMo," Freitas et al. propose an ontology to integrate the formalisms underlying agent-based systems. It provides a mechanism with which to bridge the gap between ontological knowledge bases and agent programming primitives, obviating the need to convert multiple knowledge representations into the agent programming framework. By allowing multiple ontological knowledge bases to be integrated and accessible to agent programs, the process of making inferences using much knowledge commonly available over the Internet should facilitate the achievement of a common view of the world by multiple agents. This proposal facilitates the development of applications that operate in complex scenarios, making use of knowledge intelligence to counter-balance the demand for elaborated business rules.

This development is significant in supporting the integration of data structures for the composition of intelligent recommendation systems in dynamic scenarios, such as mobile services and ambient intelligence. The work presents an illustrative scenario applying agent-based technology to monitor senior patients. The solution highlights the contribution of the technology to a real world scenario.

In the forth paper, "VIRTUAL-ME: A Library for Smart Autonomous Agents in Multiple Virtual Environments," Castano et al. present a programming tool useful to the development of smart agents that can emulate human behavior. This development is essential for creating models able to predict the evolution of social settings and for the development of computational social sciences. This development contributes with mechanisms of data and action representation of virtual worlds in specific problem domains, useful as a laboratory for the elaboration of solutions around complex reaction strategies.

In the fifth paper, "Shared Message Boards for Smart Enterprises," Shigeno et al. present an innovative form of social connectedness based on a mechanism to allow message exchange between communities. The outcome leads to a dataset of relevant research data to understand interpersonal interactions in closed communities. This information can be used to understand social behavior and networking. The paper presents a field trial in a large corporation – a form of close environment community – and analyzes the patterns around user adoption and individual and group behavior.

In the sixth paper, "On Improving Route Choice Through Learning Automata" by Ramos et al. the focus is on enabling drivers to make better route choices through intelligent agents that learn from previous routes. These intelligent automata can learn from previous routes and share information, thus allowing better route planning and decreasing congestion on already burdened transportation networks.

As in the first and second papers, this development supports technologies for collaborative services in issues of urban intelligence, in this case related to smart traffic. In addition to the contribution to intelligent recommendation systems, it promotes the creation of virtual laboratories for experimentation and analysis. This is useful to simulate complex scenarios and experiment with elaborated techniques of coordination.

In the seventh paper, "Urban Context Detection and Context-Aware Recommendation via Networks of Humans as Sensors," Alvarez-Napagao et al. propose a mechanism to infer problems that occur in everyday life by taking advantage of the geolocated positioning coming from message postings on online social networks. The proposal would allow city planners – and the population at large – to leverage the combined sensing ability of others to better understand their world.

In the eighth paper, "Mining Social Interaction Data in Virtual Worlds," Shah and Sukthankar present techniques for inferring the existence of social links from unstructured conversational data collected from groups of participants in gaming-related virtual worlds. This information can be used to understand social behavior and support innovative technologies that allow for intelligence application and collaborative services and "social labs" in virtual worlds.

In the ninth paper, "A Multi-Agent Architecture to Support Ubiquitous Applications in Smart Environments," Maciel et al. proposes a middleware architecture to support the development of applications that can integrate multiple emerging technologies such as sensor networks, social networks, cloud computing, and digital ecosystems. Related to the first paper, the proposal contributes to innovation in collaborative services for smart societies, providing the infrastructure for data collection and analyzing social phenomena in urban environments.

Finally, in the tenth paper, "Caring for My Neighborhood: A Platform for Geocoding Budget for Public Oversight," Craveiro et al. devise a method to promote citizen engagement through a better visualization of public budget expenditures. This is a significant contribution to social connectedness in smart societies and a practical application of technology to understand the macro-level activities that influence the social phenomena in urban spaces.

We must thank all the volunteers who made the workshops possible by helping to organize and by peer reviewing the submissions.

December 2014   Fernando Koch
                                                          Felipe Meneguzzi
                                                          Kiran Lakkaraju

Organization

CARE 2014

General Chairs

Fernando Koch — SAMSUNG Research Institute, Brazil
Felipe Meneguzzi — Pontificia Universidade Catolica
do Rio Grande do Sul (PUC-RS), Brazil

Steering Committee

Christian Guttmann — IBM Research, Australia
Frank Dignum — Utrecht University, Utrecht, The Netherlands
Michael Luck — King's College, London University, UK

Program Committee

Sherif Abdallah — British University, UK
Priscilla Avegliano — IBM Research, Brazil
Sergio Borger — IBM Research, Brazil
Carlos Cardonha — IBM Research, Brazil
Frank Dignum — Utrecht University, The Netherlands
Andrew Koster — SAMSUNG Research Institute, Brazil
Michael Luck — King's College London, UK
David Morley — SRI International, USA
Sascha Ossowski — Rey Juan Carlos University, Spain
Fabio Piva — SAMSUNG Research Institute, Brazil
Jan Richter — IBM Research, Australia
Onn Shehory — IBM Research, Australia
Kent Steer — IBM Research
Ingo J. Timm — University of Trier, Germany
M. Birna Van Riemsdijk — TU Delft, The Netherlands
Neil Yorke-Smith — American University of Beirut, Lebanon
Wayne Wobcke — University of New South Wales, Australia

AVSA 2014

General Chair

Kiran Lakkaraju — Sandia National Labs, USA

Organizing Committee

Gita Sukthankar — University of Central Florida, USA
Muhammad Aurangzeb Ahmad — University of Minnesota, USA

Program Committee

Christian Bauckhage	University of Bonn, Germany
Frank Dignum	Utrecht University, The Netherlands
Mohamed Elidrisi	University of Minnesota, USA
Jina Lee	Sandia National Labs, USA
Winter Mason	Facebook, USA
Il-Chul Moon	KAIST, South Korea
Jon Whetzel	Sandia National Labs, USA
Amogh Mahapatra	University of Minnesota, USA

Table of Contents

An Ubiquitous Service-Oriented Architecture for Urban Sensing

Carlos O. Rolim[1], Anubis G. Rossetto[1], Valderi R.Q. Leithardt[1,2],
Guilherme A. Borges[1], Tatiana F.M. dos Santos[3], Adriano M. Souza[3],
and Cláudio F.R. Geyer[1]

[1] Institute of Informatics, Federal University of Rio Grande do Sul, Brazil
{carlos.oberdan,agmrossetto,valderi.quietinho,gaborges,geyer}inf.ufrgs.br
[2] Group Parallel Distributed Processing and Intelligent, Institute of Technology
National Service of Industrial Training (SENAI), Brazil
valderi.leithardsenairs.org.br
[3] Postgraduate Program in Production Engineering,
Federal University of Santa Maria, Brazil
taty.nanda@gmail.com, amsouza@ufsm.br

Abstract. In the transformation from traditional to smart cities, there is an increasing trend around the world towards intelligent dynamic infrastructures that provide citizens with new services that can improve their quality of life and fulfill the criteria of energy efficiency and sustainability. In the light of this, an important challenge is how to enable citizens and cities to promote the sensing of data with regard to a number of different factors. This paper outlines the early stages of our research which is concerned with an ubiquitous service-oriented architecture for urban sensing called UrboSenti. The proposed approach differs from other sensing plat-forms since it provides a set of services to collect data from several sources and assists in the development of new sensing applications. In addition, our model encompasses all the sensing activities, ranging from the collection of data to the generation of reports about events in the city.

Keywords: Urban Sensing, Smart Cities, Service-oriented architecture, Ubiquitous.

1 Introduction

The urbanization of cities has been increasing dramatically in the last few years and it is expected that this migration of people to urban areas will continue [4]. For this reason, the question of how to meet the goals set by this socioeconomic development and thus ensure the residents' quality of life, has become a complex matter. The concept of Smart Cities is a response to this challenge [14].

According to [12], Smart Cities are urban systems that use Information and Communication Technologies (ICT) to provide an infrastructure and public services within a more interactive, accessible and efficient city. The authors point out that the predictions of a further rise in the urban population (about 70% by

F. Koch et al. (Eds.): CARE/AVSA 2014, CCIS 498, pp. 1–10, 2015.
© Springer-Verlag Berlin Heidelberg 2015

2050) has led to the emergence of the concept of Smart Cities. As a result, it is not only necessary to provide new types of services to assist in the organization of the city and the welfare of its residents, but also to offer sustainable alternatives, which can reduce the consumption of natural energy resources, and the emission of harmful gases in the atmosphere, by the use of renewable energy.

As can be seen, the concept of Smart Cities involves different areas. The final report of the "European Smart Cities" project [10] suggests that there are six factors that should be taken into account in this context: economics, governance, people, mobility, natural resources and quality of life. In all of these, it is clear that technology plays an important role as a tool-based means of arriving at solutions for inherently complex urban scenarios.

In view of this, researchers are raising important questions about how to foster citizen participation and community involvement to achieve a better interaction with the urban ecosystem. Among these initiatives, social urban sensing applications are a promising way to bring the computational world and community closer together.

In this paper, we outline the early stages of our research on an Ubiquitous Service-Oriented Architecture for Urban Sensing called UrboSenti. Our approach differs from other sensing solutions by providing a set of distributed services to collect data from several sources and assisting in the development of new sensing applications. Moreover, our model combines social sensing with traditional sensing and encompasses all the sensing activities, ranging from the collection of data to obtaining a high-level view of events in the city.

In summary, this paper adopts a seminal approach to urban sensing by employing an innovative ubiquitous service-based architecture. In addition to being original, it signals the way that further research can be carried out in this area.

This paper is structured as follows: The next section provides an overview of related work; Section 3 describes the motivational scenario and raises some of the current computational challenges; Section 4 describes the proposed architecture, and, finally, in Section 5 some conclusions are reached, together with recommendations for future research.

2   Related Work

In the literature, there are a number of key studies in urban sensing area.

In AnonySense [15,5], there is a framework for opportunistic and participatory sensing with a strong emphasis on privacy. This adopts a polling model for task dis-tribution to anonymize the location of the mobile device within the infrastructure. Furthermore, tasks are written by means of a domain-specific language called AnonyTL, which makes use of predicates based on the context of the mobile device, such as location and whether the device is moving or not.

Medusa [13] is a programming framework that provides a programming language and a distributed runtime system with a focus on crowd-sensing. This seeks to provide a common platform to carry out any kind of task supported by smartphone sensors. Medusa achieves this by employing a programming language based on XML, called Med-Script. It also specifies the workflow of sensing tasks that will be performed in smartphones (workers) that are coordinated with cloud services.

PRISM [7] provides a mobile phone sensing platform that can facilitate the development of large-scale sensing applications. PRISM seeks to address some issues of security, privacy and scalability, together with concerns about controlling the resource access in smartphones.

MobiSens [16] is concerned with the design, implementation and evaluation of a flexible platform for mobile sensing. It can be used on an individual scale (e.g. monitoring the falls of elderly people) or with community and public scales (e.g. collecting data from participants to infer collective behavior). Furthermore, MobiSens seeks to meet some of the common requirements made by these types of applications, such as privacy, energy optimization, interaction between the server and mobile client and recognition, segmentation and annotation activities.

Pogo [2] proposes a middleware infrastructure for mobile phone sensing to facilitate the construction and testing of large-scale sensing applications. Furthermore, Pogo enables the granularity of resources to be controlled at user-level to protect the privacy of volunteers. It uses the XMPP protocol to disseminate data sets.

Micro-blog [9] is responsible for the design and implementation of an application, that can allow smartphone equipped users to generate and share multimedia content data called microblogs. This kind of data can be browsed or queried through Internet map services so that different information can be obtained about stored data.

MetroSense [8] is an architecture for large-scale urban sense services that adopts an approach of opportunistic sensing networks. It takes advantage of its interaction with mobile devices and provides coordination between mobile and static people-centric sensors. On the basis of this analysis, it can be noted that all the studies examined are involved with the area of urban sensing. However, most of them only perform sensing by means of mobile phones (smartphones), and fail to carry out this task with a mix of different source, such as mobile and fixed devices. The only work that addresses other devices is MetroSense, but unlike our approach, this does not consider data from social networks.

AnonySense has a large overhead arising from the use of the pull-model. This ensures more privacy for the device than the push-model, but does not scale very well in large-scale applications. Nonetheless, the process of anonymizing data used by AnonySense and PRISM is a desirable characteristic for crowd-sensing applications that need to publish public data in an anonymous way; however, it is not suitable for all types of systems such as healthcare and personal sensing services. In our work, these issues are not intrinsically bound to the core of the platform. Instead, we provide a set of services for this purpose so that the developer can use it when required.

Moreover, most of the works support both opportunistic and participatory sensing, as is the case with our approach (the exceptions are Medusa and Micro-blog that only address participatory sensing, and in contrast, MetroSense that only supports opportunistic sensing). However, only AnonySene and MetroSense consider the use of Delay-Tolerant Networks (DTNs) as a paradigm for situations where the infrastructure is not available. In our platform, support will be provided for both opportunistic and participatory sensing with the use of several communications paradigms, including DTN.

Furthermore, a key area where our approach differs from all the others is the usage of Service-Oriented Architecture (SOA) to design the services and components. This provides more flexibility for integration than the other current solutions, by reducing the complexity of the proposed platform and leveraging the reusability of the existing services to find new solutions rather than trying to re-invent the wheel. Finally, it should be highlighted that all the works focus on gathering sensing data. However, none of them is concerned about providing a complete solution for collecting and analyzing data or giving people feedback. It is our belief that we are filling this gap by providing a platform that covers all these stages.

3   Application Scenario

Our research has been driven by the problem-scenario that is shown in Fig. 1. This scenario includes a city with several data sources that are being used for sensing. Human-carried, fixed or vehicle-mounted sensors are applied for obtaining sensing maps of transits, air quality, noise levels, temperature, CO_2 concentration, etc. Moreover, data from social networks are used in conjunction with sensors data to provide a holistic view of the city.

The scenario in the diagram considers an urban sensing ecosystem where the following computational challenges have to be addressed: (i) heterogeneous devices (both fixed and mobile) are used to collect data and access the resulting processed information. (ii) context-aware and adaptation mechanisms are needed to support the application adaptation; (iii) a large amount of data is continuously being generated and collected throughout the city. This requires high processing power, with data preferably being processed in real time; (iv) uncertainty about whether the collected data require data fusion and analytics techniques to generated useful and correct information for decision-making and to allow it to be exported to other systems; (v) the infrastructure for communications is not always available. This require an alternative means of inter-device communication, like ad-hoc networks or delay tolerant networks; (vi) data security of the collected data and privacy for the citizens and devices used by sensing; (vii) the possibility of reusing the software components so that new sensing applications can be deployed. The computational challenges listed above are based on findings from researchers such as [4,1,11,6,3]. They observed an increasing demand for new ubiquitous and pervasive solutions to provide better services for citizens in a Smart City.

With this in mind, we argue that an ubiquitous service-oriented architecture could provide a set of components and services that can meet all the challenges (i to vii) mentioned earlier. In the next section, we will state our views about this architecture.

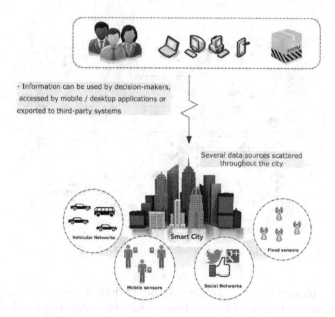

Fig. 1. Problem scenario

4   Proposed Architecture

In this section there will be an examination of an architecture called UrboSenti. UrboSenti is a term that originates from the combination of two Esperantos words: Urbo = urban, city and Senti = feel, sense. We settled on this name, because we want-ed to represent the idea of a computational solution that is able to "feel the pulse" of the city.

Figure 2 provides a high-level view of UrboSenti which involves collecting data from the city, reasoning about them and providing feedback to citizens and other systems. We are adopting a Service Oriented Architecture (SOA) approach to guide our design. In this way, we are able to avoid using well-defined tiers (or layers), since this kind of traditional approach would constrain the value and flexibility of the functionalities of the modules, and thus result in dependencies across the unrelated components. Instead, we designed our architecture in services. This is the SOA mode of revealing the functionalities of the components used by other components or modules, and ensures flexibility and reusability.

Our architecture is split into two key modules: the *Sensing module* and *Backend module*.

The heart and brain of UrboSenti is the *Backend module*. It runs in a data center infrastructure and, in short, is responsible for receiving sensed data, processing it and giving feedback to the citizens and other systems.

Its internal components and services are outlined in Figure 3 and its behavior is explained below.

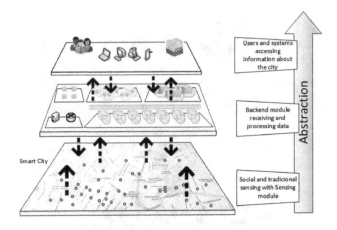

Fig. 2. High-level view of UrboSenti

- **Services Repository:** aggregates all the services available. The services are grouped into categories in accordance with their objectives and those services available are: (i) Data services: used to handle all the data employed by the architecture. It also provides services to retrieve and store data and functionalities as well as to "clean" the collected data from inconsistencies and noise; (ii) Social services: services related to the handling of the relevant data from social networks; (iii) Sensing services: services to interface with

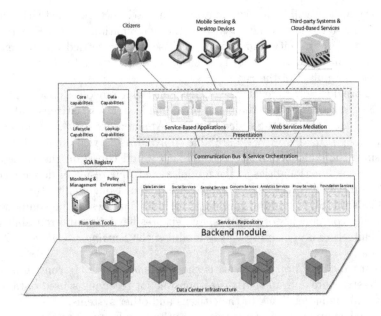

Fig. 3. Backend module

different sensors and aggregate collected data. Its use supports open standards to facilitate data exchange; (iv) Concern services: used to deal with issues of security, encryption and the privacy of data and users; (v) Analytics services: services for mining, classification and reports. In addition to obtaining information, these services are able to correlate data from different sources and predict events in the city; (vi) Proxy services: services to interact with external systems like vehicular or sensor networks and to exchange data with third-party systems; (vii) Foundation services: these comprise all the basic services.

- **Communication Bus and Services Orchestration:** this is the bus used for inter-components communication. It also carries out, the coordination and arrangement of calls and invocations for multiple services so that they can be viewed as a single aggregated service.
- **Web Services Mediation:** this is an intermediary system between external entities, like sensing devices and third-party systems, and Services Repository (invoked by Communication Bus & Service Orchestration components).
- **Service-Based Applications:** all the applications that are built by aggregating the available services from the architecture. Together with *Web Services Mediation*, this composes the most external component of the architecture, called Presentation, which interacts with the users and other systems.
- **SOA Registry:** this it is an identity-management system for available services. Its internal services keep track of the metadata on the services, which give each service a single identity. The information stored for each service establishes ownership for the service and specifies how the service behaves at run time (the lifecycle of the service). It also provides artifacts to handle the UDDI data store and services registry/lookup.
- **Run Time Tools:** these comprise the tools required for the monitoring and management of the services. They contain artifacts generated at run time, such as logged messages, archived performance data, archived health, and the heartbeat of the main components, as well as providing Key Performance Indicators (KPIs) for dashboards and reports of service performance. The Policy Enforcement ensures that the messages are properly formed and that the services are executed properly and are in compliance with service-level agreements.

The other main module of UrboSenti is called *Sensing module*. This module is re-sponsible for social and traditional sensing and encompasses activities of intentional and non-intentional sensing. It runs in mobile devices (e.g. mobile phones, embedded in vehicles, etc) and in fixed sensors scattered around the city. The internal compo-nents are depicted in Figure 4 and its behavior is explained below. It should be stressed that these components are composed of other subcomponents to provide internal services, but these have been omitted for reasons of clarity and limited space.

- **Micro-kernel:** The core of this module. Its main function is to provide basic services for more external components. Internally, the Micro-kernel is

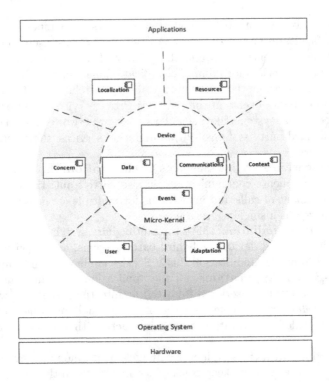

Fig. 4. Sensing module

structured in the following: (i) The Device: this provides basic information about the running device (name, network address, interfaces, GPS, internal sensors, etc); (ii) Communications: this provides methods to send and receive messages by means of the available network infrastructure, such as IEEE 802.11b/g/n (structured and ad-hoc), GPRS/EDGE/3G and Ethernet as the underlying system for TCP/UDP communications. When the network infrastructure is not available, this module provides support for a Delay Tolerant Network approach via Bluetooth interface; (iii) Data: handling operations for storing and retrieving data; (iv) Events: capturing external events of interest (a positional change due to a users movement, alteration of interface status, etc). The detected events are available for use by other components.

- **Localization:** handling localization issues such as geopositioning information, Points Of Interest (POI) and Location Based Services (LBS).
- **Resources:** set of components and services for monitoring local resources and discovering resources from other devices
- **Concern:** handling security, privacy and encryption issues.
- **Context:** group components and methods for context-awareness (i.e. context reasoning, context knowledge, context discovery, context prediction)
- **User:** handling the users preferences, social networks profiles and basic knowledge of the user.

- **Adaptation:** components and services to make adaptations to the behavior of the device. This employs a set of policies and knowledge to describe how to adapt the application and monitor basic quality of service data to infer when the adaptation is needed.

At the top is the Application layer which represents the sensing applications. At lower layers, are Operating System and the Hardware of the device.

The development of UrboSenti has been started. Currently we are mainly working on the Sensing module, or more specifically on the Micro-kernel. The basic functionalities of all the internal modules, except the Communications module, have been carried out. We are coding this module so that several network interfaces can be used to send and receive data in accordance with the existing infrastructure. We already have support for TCP/UDP communications with the aid of the wireless and wired infrastructure. However, we are stuck with Bluetooth communication used in Delay Tolerant Networks paradigm. At this stage, we are facing difficulties about paring new devices in suitable time and exchanging information with existing devices without timing out. However, we hope to solve this issue soon so that we can be in a position to start coding the external components of the Sensing module. After this, our focus will be on the Backend module. This module has a good deal of coding material and requires a long time to be carried out. In other words, we have a hard task to ensure that the two main modules will be able to exchange data and that the pro-posed platform can be used in a real scenario.

5   Conclusions and Future Work

In this paper, we have described the early stages of our attempts to build a new ubiquitous service oriented architecture for urban sensing called UrboSenti. We have also outlined our initial design for the software modules, their internal components and the provided services. The proposal has one significant difference from that of other researchers, which is that our approach is able to fill the gap that has been left by related studies and addresses the computational challenges raised by our initial problem-scenario. Moreover, this should encourage us to conduct further research into the multidisciplinary area of Smart Cities with the aim of improving services and applications for urban sensing.

As way of making a step forward in this research, it is worth highlighting the need for the proposed modules to be encoded and to find a way to simulate the implementation before it is put in a real test-bed.

Acknowledgments. This research was supported by the UbiArch project - Ubiquitous Architecture for Context Management and Application Development at UFRGS.

References

1. Boyle, D.E., Yates, D.C., Yeatman, E.M.: Urban Sensor Data Streams: London 2013. IEEE Internet Computing 17(6), 12–20 (2013)
2. Brouwers, N., Langendoen, K.: Pogo, a Middleware for Mobile Phone Sensing. In: Narasimhan, P., Triantafillou, P. (eds.) Middleware 2012. LNCS, vol. 7662, pp. 21–40. Springer, Heidelberg (2012)
3. Cardone, G., Foschini, L., Bellavista, P., Corradi, A., Borcea, C., Talasila, M., Curtmola, R.: Fostering participaction in smart cities: A geo-social crowdsensing platform. IEEE Communications Magazine 51(6), 112–119 (2013)
4. Celino, I., Kotoulas, S.: Smart Cities [Guest editors' introduction]. IEEE Internet Computing 17(6), 8–11 (2013)
5. Cornelius, C., Kapadia, A., Kotz, D., Peebles, D., Shin, M., Triandopoulos, N.: AnonySense: Privacy-Aware People-Centric Sensing Categories and Subject Descriptors. In: MobiSys 2008 - Proceeding of the 6th International Conference on Mobile Systems, Applications, and Services, Colorado, USA (2008)
6. Crang, M., Graham, S.: Sentient cities: Ambient intelligence and the politics of urban space. Information Communication Society 10(6), 789–817 (2007)
7. Das, T., Mohan, P., Padmanabhan, V.N., Ramjee, R., Sharma, A.: PRISM: Platform for remote sensing using smartphones. In: Proceedings of the 8th International Conference on Mobile Systems, Applications, and Services, MobiSys 2010, pp. 63–76. ACM Press, New York (2010)
8. Eisenman, S.B., Lane, N.D., Miluzzo, E., Peterson, R.A., Ahn, G.S., Campbell, A.T.: MetroSense Project: People-Centric Sensing at Scale. In: Proc. of Workshop on World-Sensor-Web (WSW 2006), Boulder, pp. 6–11 (2006)
9. Gaonkar, S., Li, J., Choudhury, R.R., Cox, L., Schmidt, A.: Micro-Blog: Sharing and querying content through mobile phones and social participation. In: Proceeding of the 6th International Conference on Mobile Systems, Applications, and Services, MobiSys 2008, pp. 174–186. ACM Press, New York (2008)
10. Giffinger, R., Fertner, C., Kramar, H., Kalasek, R.: Smart Cities - Ranking of European Medium-Sized Cities. Tech. rep., Vienna University of Technology, Viena (2007)
11. Koch, F.L.: An Agent-Based Model for the Development of Intelligent Mobile Services. Phd thesis, University Utrecht (UU) (2009)
12. Pellicer, S., Santa, G., Bleda, A.L., Maestre, R., Jara, A.J., Skarmeta, A.G.: A Global Perspective of Smart Cities: A Survey. In: 2013 Seventh International Conference on Innovative Mobile and Internet Services in Ubiquitous Computing, pp. 439–444 (July 2013)
13. Ra, M.R., Liu, B., La Porta, T.F., Govindan, R.: Medusa: A Programming Framework for Crowd-Sensing Applications. In: Proceedings of the 10th International Conference on Mobile Systems, Applications, and Services, MobiSys 2012, p. 337, No. Section 2. ACM Press, New York (2012)
14. Schaffers, H., Komninos, N., Pallot, M., Trousse, B.: Smart Cities and the Future Internet: Towards Cooperation Frameworks for Open Innovation. In: Domingue, J., et al. (eds.) Future Internet Assembly. LNCS, vol. 6656, pp. 431–446. Springer, Heidelberg (2011)
15. Shin, M., Cornelius, C., Peebles, D., Kapadia, A., Kotz, D., Triandopoulos, N.: AnonySense: A system for anonymous opportunistic sensing. Pervasive and Mobile Computing 7(1), 16–30 (2011)
16. Wu, P., Zhu, J., Zhang, J.Y.: MobiSens: A Versatile Mobile Sensing Platform for Real-World Applications. Mobile Networks and Applications 18(1), 60–80 (2012)

Geo-fencing Based Disaster Management Service

Piotr Szczytowski

NEC Laboratories Europe, Heidelberg, Germany
piotr.szczytowski@neclab.eu

Abstract. The success of disaster handling often depends on the efficient flow of information. The social media and networks receive a growing attention as potential source of valuable data in disaster scenarios. The social network based information flow is real-time, direct, two-directional and often geo-tagged. Unfortunately, besides these obvious advantages, social network data suffers from drawbacks: it is unstructured, dispersed and lacks reliability. This paper proposes an approach based on combining a geo-fencing technology with social network platform to combat this problem and deliver a novel service for disaster management. The service groups users ad-hoc based on their location. Social network features allow users to exchange real-time information, coordinate rescue efforts, issue and report tasks. The geo-fences are visualized to provide a good overview of the disaster zone. The service was evaluated by disaster management experts, with an encouraging feedback.

1 Introduction

The time and place of disasters in most instances is hardly foreseeable. The proper preparation for disaster events is very important but despite much invested effort it cannot handle all circumstances of the disaster. Successful tackling of the disaster largely depends on the proper flow of information. The disaster related information can be hard to gather and incomplete in emergency situation. It was already demonstrated [14, 3] that in disaster scenarios the information gathered locally, especially form affected communities, is of particular importance. One of the possibilities to get an access to the local information is by crowd sourcing [5, 1]. The social networks paradigm can serve as a rich and valuable source of crowd sourced information. The main advantages of the information flow in social networks is the fact that the information is provided in real-time, moreover it is direct and two-directional. In many instances the information is also geo-tagged, thanks to prevalence of mobile devices equipped with GPS sensors.

The main drawback of information collected from social networks is the fact the the data is largely unstructured, dispersed and only miniscule portion of it is of significance. The first goal is then to filter the data and correlate it with the location of the disaster. In this paper, we propose an approach for dealing with this problem based on concept of combining geo-fencing technology with features of social networks.

A geo-fencing system can be described as a database which maintains the two-dimensional coordinates of mobile objects and permanently matches them

F. Koch et al. (Eds.): CARE/AVSA 2014, CCIS 498, pp. 11–21, 2015.

against a set of geo-fences (virtual perimeter), where geo-fences are the continuous version of spatial range queries.

The geo-fences can be deployed to mark an area affected by the geo-fence. Next, social network participants whose location coincides with the geo-fence can be grouped together into a dedicated disaster communication group. These can be used exclusively for purpose of broadcasting warning messages about the disaster in given locality, or for communication within the disaster zone. The occurrences of events (entrance or exit) triggered by people coming into and out of the geo-fence marked disaster zone can be used to deduct flow of people and estimate number of civilians. These geo-fences can be visualized as polygons on a map at a disaster management control center. An activity feed listing the communications and undertaken actions within the geo-fence can be attached to the polygons.

Related work. One of the straight forward approaches to handling disaster management is to employ a Geographic Information System (GIS) [17, 12]. The GIS can be in particular used for mission planing purposes along with sensor data [12], or used for purpose of risk mapping [17]. A satellite imaginary can be efficiently used for rapid mapping of the disaster zone [19]. A disaster tailored software can also be used for creating easily accessible registries for missing persons, organizations, shelters, and managing inventories [4]. Independent and not necessarily designed for disaster handling services can be dynamically combined to provide emergency services using service orchestration technology [20, 2].

Besides the dedicated disaster management software, also the social media and networking can be a valuable tool for handling emergency situations. In particular, the case study described in [6] shows how web-based tools (e.g. bulletin board system, Google maps) and social networks (e.g. Twitter) were used spontaneously by the community members to exchange information and inform rescuers about situation. The authors in [5] describe advantages (real-time, variety of data sources, and geo-tagging) of the crowd-sourced information as well as notice its shortfalls (lack of coordination, inaccuracy, security issues).

Social media technologies can be used in particular as collaboration workspaces or knowledge sharing platforms [23, 22]. Social media support "'backchannel"' communications, allowing for wide scale interaction. Information not accessible by dedicated channels becomes available thanks to wider involvement of the public [1, 18]. As an example, in [8] authors explore the concept of community response grids (CRGs), by evaluating the viability of combining the mobile technologies, web based tools and e-government to improve efficiency of information exchange and facilitate resident-to-resident assistance.

Geo-fencing has been discussed from a deployment and application point of view for about a decade. In one of the early works, Munson and Gupta have described geofencing as a "general-purpose service" and proposed an architecture for its realization on a large scale [13]. In the main body of literature on geo-fencing, applications of this technology are described in a broad variety of different domains, see [9, 10, 15, 2, 7, 16]. The geo-fences technology can also be successfully applied for disaster management. It can serve as efficient medium for localized broadcast of messages [21], or coordinating deployment of the rescue efforts which depend on the volunteers skills sets [11].

Our contribution. In this work we present a Geo-fencing based Disaster Management Service. The service combines features of social network with those of geo-fencing to deliver a novel set of tools for disaster management. Social network users are grouped ad-hoc based on they location being within confines of a geo-fence. Using social network functionalities users can exchange and disseminate information in the real-time, coordinate rescue efforts, issue and report tasks. The geo-fences are easy to visualize and provide a good overview of the in-the-field situation. The service incorporates a control center web application for the disaster management operators and a mobile application for the servicemen and civilians.

The presented design was fully implemented as a proof of concept. Three use cases that utilize the service were designed and subsequently presented within a focus group session to the disaster management experts. The experts evaluated the service during a discussion, which took place directly after the service demonstration.

2 Disaster Management Service

Before giving the detailed description of the Disaster Management Service and its features, a set of prerequisites is presented. These are provided to define necessary concepts and building blocks of the service.

2.1 Prerequisites

The service was build upon two major components, namely Societies Platform and Geo-fencing technology. Subsequent paragraphs provide details of these concepts and their interaction.

Societies. Societies is a social networking platform developed within EU funded project called Societies. The project aim is to investigate and address the gap between pervasive and social computing. To achieve its aim, the project develops a set of innovations targeted for social networking; among them: learning (acquire knowledge about user by monitoring their actions over time), community preferences (reusable preference templates), user intent (deduce user goals based on their activities), community orchestration, community context, trust, privacy and others. Societies project targets three major user groups: enterprise users, students, and disaster relief experts. The presented in this paper service was realized as one of the Societies platform demonstrators.

Community Interaction Spaces. The Societies paradigm for modeling users associations is based on concept of Community Interaction Spaces (CIS). CIS in general represents a loose associations between users that are its members.

CIS's are described by a unique identifier, name, and description; they support dynamic membership, which depends on set of defined criteria. A set of shared services/resources can be attached to CIS, using a shared activity feed. Activity feed allows data to be posted by individual members of the group and be visible to all of its members.

Geo-fencing. Geo-fence constitutes a virtual perimeter for a real-world geographic area. The primary goal of geo-fencing service is to track events associated with crossing the boundary of the geo-fence. The service takes as an input current and previous object location coordinates and evaluates them against existing geo-fences. If the set of geo-fences for previous and current location differs, then the crossing is detected. As a result of detected crossing, the service generates a notification, which identifies the type of an event (entrance or exit), the affected geo-fence(s) and the object/user that triggered the event.

Geo-fencing and Societies. Using a geo-fencing service in conjunction with CIS concept, it is possible to design and implement a specialized CIS based on an association of geo-fence and CIS. This specialized CIS accepts as members only users that at the same time are within perimeter of a geo-fence associated with CIS. Every notification issued from geo-fencing service results in joining or leaving the respective CIS, which border was crossed. As a result the users can be made aware of the existence of CIS, while entering its boundary. Moreover, the users are able to discover presence of other users within close proximity as they are also members of CIS. Communication and sharing of the information among the users is made possible by use of the activity feed of the CIS. The CIS also stores the definition of the geo-fence, so it potentially can be reconstructed on a client mobile application and visualized.

2.2 Service Description

In case of handling disaster, the comprehensive situation overview is of paramount importance. In particular, the location of the disaster, its type, severity, the size and distribution over the affected area, and presence of people is of main interest. For the people in the proximity of the area affected by disaster it is important to receive the warning about the presence of danger and its nature. These users should also be notified when they wander into the disaster area. Also the servicemen (e.g. rescuers) on the ground should be able to easily localize the disaster and interact with the coordination team at disaster management center. In particular they should be able to modify the disaster geo-fence properties. They should also be able to directly deploy new disaster geo-fences based on current situation. The Geo-fencing based Disaster Management Service tackles these important aspects of disaster management. The service consists of two applications: Control Center Web Application and Mobile Application, which are described in following paragraphs.

Fig. 1. Architecture overview of geo-fencing based Disaster Management Service

2.3 Architecture overview

The Figure 2.3 provides an overview of the Disaster Management Service. Societies Platform is responsible for storing the state information of CIS and its activity feed (including shape of the geo-fence). Geo-fencing Server stores only the geo-fences (a set of ordered vertices) indexed using unique identifier (ID). No other information is stored, all data about CIS are kept private form the Geo-fencing Server. Mobile Application forwards GPS location to the Geo-fencing Server. If event is detected the Mobile Application receives notification and uses Societies Platform API to join/leave the CIS which ID matches that of geo-fence that triggered the event. Control Center Web Application uses Societies Platform to query existing CIS's with their activity feeds (uses feed data for visualization) and to deploy new CIS. When a new CIS is deployed, its definition is stored at Societies Platform and a geo-fence attached to CIS is stored at Geo-fencing Server. The same happens when CIS is created using Mobile Application.

Control Center Web Application. The Control Center Web Application is meant to be used by the Disaster Management Center coordination team in order to obtain a disaster situation overview. The main panel displays a map with marked on it currently deployed disaster geo-fences. The geo-fences are modeled as polygons whose coloring and transparency level correspond to the type and severity of the disaster. The operator (member or leader of coordination team) can interact with the map by selecting the polygons. Upon clicking on a polygon the interface displays additional details about the disaster area. These details include the list of the current members of the disaster geo-fence (thereby confirming their presence), the unique name of the associated with the geo-fence CIS and its description, indicator of severity as well as current content of the activity feed. The members, whose occupation identifies them as serviceman, are marked with separate color on the members list, so that the operator can easily differentiate between civilians and servicemen. The operator can modify the description of the CIS as well as its severity depending on the information from the activity feed. The operator can also post new information to the activity feed to broadcast the information to the members within disaster CIS. Apart from messages, the activity feed also contains information about the events of joining and leaving the CIS.

Moreover, the operator can use activity feed to assign a task to CIS. A task describes a set of activities that should be performed by servicemen while within the disaster geo-fence. The tasks are visible only to the servicemen and appear as special notification upon entering the geo-fence or upon they initial issuance by the operator.

The Web Application also allows the operator to create a new disaster CIS, for example based on reconnaissance photos from disaster area. It is done as easily as drawing a polygon on the map. Next, an additional information is provided, which includes unique name, initial description, type of disaster and its severity. Once disaster CIS is deployed the mobile application users will be notified while crossing its boundary. The Web Application will also try to query for the context based user location information. If user permits access to it, and his/hers location falls into CIS defined geo-fence, then the user will be added to CIS already upon creation. After the disaster situation is resolved the operator can delete respective disaster CIS. For this purpose, the operator just selects proper polygon form the map and chooses the delete option.

Mobile Application. The mobile application is designed to work with Android OS. The application is typically running in the background (so the user can still work with other applications) and is sending current user location for evaluation to the geo-fencing service. The current location can be either obtained from the internal GPS sensor of the smartphone (then used to update context location), or if the GPS signal is unavailable (i.e. inside the building) then the Societies context information can be used as a location source. The mobile application also subscribes to the notifications form geo-fencing service. Upon receiving a notification the application acts upon it by joining or leaving disaster CIS which boundary the user just crossed. The join operation is accompanied with bringing the application to focus and an additional notification displayed on the screen of the smartphone. The form of notification (vibration, sound, task bar notification, dialog window) and its content depends on the severity and type of disaster respectively. Moreover, the user whose occupation is designated as a serviceman may use the application to deploy a new geo-fence to mark a disaster that s/he just spotted. The interface allows defining type of the disaster, its severity, unique name, basic description, location, radius of the affected area and its orientation (relative to user location). The serviceman may also modify properties (description and severity) of already deployed disaster CIS if s/he is its member. Independent of the user occupation each member of the disaster CIS can read the details of the CIS as well as is able to read and post new messages to the CIS activity feed.

In case of a serviceman using the mobile application, the application will also show notifications about tasks assigned to geo-fences that the serviceman is co-located with. The serviceman after executing the task may use the application to post a report to the task. This will change the status of the task to completed and will also appear in the activity feed visible by the operator at the Control Center.

Fig. 2. Control Center screen-shot

Fig. 3. Mobile Application screen-shots

3   Trial and Evaluation

The service as described in previous section was subjected to the trial, which involved disaster experts. First, the description of use cases demonstrated to the experts is given, next a feedback received during the discussion is presented.

3.1   Use Case 1: Deployment and Visualization

In this use case, a disaster is either reported over the phone to the Control Center, or alternatively a feedback from air reconnaissance is provided regarding a disaster underway. Based on the available information, the operator uses Web Application to draw a polygon marking the potential location and shape of disaster area. Also information about type and severity of the disaster are provided. Upon creating a disaster geo-fence, it is displayed on the situation map. The users (including servicemen) already within the confines of the disaster geo-fence, join the associated CIS and receive notification about nature and severity of disaster. The operator, after short moment can estimate number of civilians present in the danger zone, and number of already available servicemen. The operator can now also assign task to the disaster geo-fence as to instruct the in-field servicemen i.e. to evacuate the civilians.

3.2   Use Case 2: In the Field Deployment and Coordination

This use case demonstrates how the servicemen in the field can use the mobile application to report a disaster. A servicemen equipped with the mobile application upon spotting a disaster, can use the application to deploy a disaster geo-fence. The application allows to define name, description, type and severity of the disaster. The location of the deployed disaster geo-fence is the location that the mobile application obtains directly form the on-board GPS sensor. The user can influence the shape and size of the disaster geo-fence, by specifying radius size of the geo-fence, as well its orientation (center, north, east, etc...) in respect to the users current location. Immediately after deployment, the disaster geo-fence shows-up in the Control Center Web Application as a polygon with a coloring and transparency corresponding to the type and severity of the disaster. The operator upon selecting the polygon can inspect further details and the activity feed for messages from servicemen.

The servicemen can also use geo-fences and associated with them tasks to coordinate the rescue effort. In a situation where there are multiple localities requiring attention, the servicemen can deploy for each locality separate smaller geo-fences and assign to them tasks. Now, servicemen newly arriving at the disaster zone, upon entering the geo-fence can track the tasks and reports to determine whether they presence is still required at given locality or if they should move to next one where no personnel is present yet.

3.3   Use Case 3: Peer-to-Peer Geo-fencing

This use case illustrates a potential of using geo-fencing technology in the context of the civilian. In this instance the geo-fence not necessarily represents a disaster, but i.e. an injury on part of the civilian. A civilian in secluded area like forest, upon incurring injury which renders him unable to move, may use a geo-fence to alert possibly nearby civilians or serviceman about his condition. Upon deploying geo-fence, other users equipped with mobile application will receive notification about being within a geo-fence, which marks a call for help. The serviceman being in close proximity may arrive much faster than the emergency services that were alerted using the emergency number. The serviceman can use the activity feed to message the injured that the help is on the way. Moreover, also the emergency service operator using the visualization tool will also be aware of the location of emergency and the fact that a serviceman is already present. In such situation the operator can reschedule emergency deployment to higher priority events where no serviceman is yet present.

3.4   Trial

The trial was evaluated by employing the focus groups method. The use cases were presented to two focus groups. First focus group included representatives form the civil defense, fire department and mounted search and rescue organization (one representative per each organization). The second group included representatives form Irish police (An Garda Sochna) (three representatives). After the presentation of the use cases an open discussion was initiated. Experts shared their initial impressions of the presented technologies with anecdotes and references to their real world experiences. The presented service and use cases received a very good reception from both focus groups. The functionalities provided by the service were in general well recognized, and participants themselves postulated possible applications of the service, along with ideas for new enhanced functions and some improvements to the existing ones.

Among the features that gathered most interest were, the visualization capabilities to represent the disaster on the map along with the information provided by the activity feed. Equally valuable rated was the possibility of in-the-field deployment of geo-fences for signaling and mapping of events. The service was also seen as a good tool for after action evaluation and verification. One of the expert recognized additional possibility to use the geo-fences to mark regions of varying severity, and later depending on the presence of the servicemen in the zone, to sent them for decontamination if needed. It was also proposed to use the geo-fences not only to mark a disaster zone, but also to deploy geo-fences tagged as a 'safe-zone'. These would be used to let the people, fleeing from disaster, know that their have reached a safe spot. This principle was also proposed to use for marking areas where an important rescue operation equipment is stored (e.g. defibrillator).

The Geo-fencing based service was also seen very favorably as good source of crowd-sourced data. The Irish police group indicated some lack of security features (e.g. how to handle situation when a smartphone with the mobile application used by a serviceman is stolen by a criminal), however those were not the focus of the demonstration. Finally a representative of civil defense issued an open invitation for participation in a large scale in-the-field trial of the service in August 2014.

4   Future Work

We foresee further extensions for the presented disaster management service. One of the functionalities that we identified that could increase usability of the service is to introduce posting of photos to the activity feed, so they would be visible along the messages. Another feature asked for is more robust filtering depending on source of message in the activity feed (e.g. showing only messages from a given serviceman). On the side of geo-fencing we would like to add support for mobile geo-fencing, where it could be utilized to model movement of the disaster zones (e.g. in cases of floods, strong winds, etc...). Finally, we are considering possibility of automatic deployment of geo-fences based on the geo-tagged measurement data collected from in-the-field sensors, or based on analysis of the content of Facebook/Twitter posts.

5   Summary and Conclusion

The merge of two concepts, namely Community Interaction Space (CIS) and geo-fencing, results in an effective tool for handling of the disaster management. The grouping of users based on their geographic location allows easier and more efficient communication (e.g. localized message broadcasting) and situation mapping (map based visualization). The deployment of geo-fences offers dual functionality of warning as well as of coordinating rescue effort.

The disaster management service trial with participation of the disaster experts served as validation of the presented concept but also as a source of new ideas about possible use cases for the service and new features that can be integrated for increased service usability.

Acknowledgments. This paper describes work undertaken in the context of the projects *Self Orchestrating CommunIty ambiEnT IntelligEnce Spaces (Societies)* - http://www.ict-societies.eu/ and *MobiNet* - http://www.mobinet. eu/. Societies and MobiNet are Large Scale Collaborative Projects supported by the European 7th Framework Programme under the contract numbers 257493 and 318485 respectively.

References

[1] Backchannels on the front lines: Emergency uses of social media in the 2007 Southern California wildfires. University of Colorado (2008)

[2] Bareth, U., Kupper, A., Ruppel, P.: Geoxmart-a marketplace for geofence-based mobile services. In: 2010 IEEE 34th Annual Computer Software and Applications Conference (COMPSAC), pp. 101–106. IEEE (2010)

[3] Buckland, J., Rahman, M.: Community-based disaster management during the 1997 red river flood in canada. Disasters 23(2), 174–191 (1999)

[4] Currion, P., de Silva, C., Van de Walle, B.: Open source software for disaster management. Commun. ACM 50(3), 61–65 (2007)

[5] Gao, H., Barbier, G., Goolsby, R.: Harnessing the crowdsourcing power of social media for disaster relief. IEEE Intelligent Systems 26(3), 10–14 (2011)

[6] Huang, C.-M., Chan, E., Hyder, A.: Web 2.0 and internet social networking: A new tool for disaster management? - lessons from taiwan. BMC Medical Informatics and Decision Making 10(1), 57 (2010)

[7] Ijeh, A.C., Brimicombe, A.J., Preston, D.S., Imafidon, C.O.: Geofencing in a Security Strategy Model. In: Jahankhani, H., Hessami, A.G., Hsu, F. (eds.) ICGS3 2009. CCIS, vol. 45, pp. 104–111. Springer, Heidelberg (2009)

[8] Jaeger, P.T., Shneiderman, B., Fleischmann, K.R., Preece, J., Qu, Y., Wu, P.F.: Community response grids: E-government, social networks, and effective emergency management. Telecommun. Policy 31(10-11), 592–604 (2007)

[9] Küpper, A., Bareth, U., Freese, B.: Geofencing and background tracking–the next features in LBSs. In: Proceedings of the 41th Annual Conference of the Gesellschaft für Informatik eV (2011)

[10] Martin, D., Alzua, A., Lamsfus, C.: A contextual geofencing mobile tourism service. In: Information and Communication Technologies in Tourism 2011, pp. 191–202. Springer (2011)

[11] Meyers, R.C.: System for establishing geo-fence for dispersing volunteer skill sets, US Patent App. 13/289,991 (May 10, 2012)

[12] Montoya, L.: Geo-data acquisition through mobile GIS and digital video: An urban disaster management perspective. Environmental Modelling & Software, Integrating Environmental Modelling and GI-Technology 18(10), 869–876, (2003)

[13] Munson, J.P., Gupta, V.K.: Location-based notification as a general-purpose service. In: Proceedings of the 2nd International Workshop on Mobile Commerce, pp. 40–44. ACM (2002)

[14] Nakagawa, Y., Shaw, R.: Social capital: A missing link to disaster recovery

[15] Reclus, F., Drouard, K.: Geofencing for fleet & freight management. In: 2009 9th International Conference on Intelligent Transport Systems Telecommunications (ITST), pp. 353–356. IEEE (2009)

[16] Schneider, G., Dreher, B., Seidel, O.: Using geofencing as a means to support flexible real time applications for delivery services. In: 5th International Workshop on Ubiquitous Computing (IWUC 2008), Barcelona, Spain (2008)

[17] Tran, P., Shaw, R., Chantry, G., Norton, J.: Gis and local knowledge in disaster management: A case study of flood risk mapping in viet nam. Disasters 33(1), 152–169 (2009)

[18] Underwood, S.: Improving disaster management. Commun. ACM 53(2), 18–20 (2010)

[19] Voigt, S., Kemper, T., Riedlinger, T., Kiefl, R., Scholte, K., Mehl, H.: Satellite image analysis for disaster and crisis-management support. IEEE Transactions on Geoscience and Remote Sensing 45(6), 1520–1528 (2007)

[20] Weiser, A., Zipf, A.: Web service orchestration of ogc web services for disaster management. In: Li, J., Zlatanova, S., Fabbri, A. (eds.) Geomatics Solutions for Disaster Management. Lecture Notes in Geoinformation and Cartography, pp. 239–254. Springer, Heidelberg (2007)

[21] Weiser, D., Wood, M.A., Preston, K.R.: Message broadcasting geo-fencing system and method, US Patent 7,801,538 (September 21, 2010)

[22] White, C., Plotnick, L., Kushma, J., Hiltz, S.R., Turoff, M.: An online social network for emergency management. International Journal of Emergency Management 6(3-1), 369–382 (2010)

[23] Yates, D., Paquette, S.: Emergency knowledge management and social media technologies: A case study of the 2010 haitian earthquake. International Journal of Information Management 31(1), 6–13 (2011)

Applying Ontologies and Agent Technologies to Generate Ambient Intelligence Applications

Artur Freitas, Daniela Schmidt, Alison Panisson,
Rafael H. Bordini, Felipe Meneguzzi, and Renata Vieira

Pontifical Catholic University of Rio Grande do Sul - PUCRS
Postgraduate Programme in Computer Science, School of Informatics (FACIN)
Porto Alegre - RS - Brazil
{artur.freitas,daniela.schmidt,alison.panisson}@acad.pucrs.br,
{rafael.bordini,felipe.meneguzzi,renata.vieira}@pucrs.br

Abstract. The specification of agent systems comprises different dimensions normally defined using distinct formalisms. Since this lack of a uniform representation makes harder to express how each level affects the others, we propose an ontology to integrate the formalisms that originally cover a single multi-agent system dimension. In doing this, we align semantic technologies and knowledge representation for agents, environments, and organisations providing agent-oriented designers with a unified approach for developing complex systems. In our approach, we represent the abstractions typical of each multi-agent system dimension as an ontology, and we exemplify both the use of such ontologies to model an eldercare application in the context of ambient intelligence and smart cities, as well as how the ontology concepts support coding in agent platforms. We discuss the implications of such integrated view for designing agents, and highlight its advantages for agent-based software development.

Keywords: ontology, multi-agent system, ambient intelligence.

1 Introduction

The use of ontologies in the context of Multi-Agent Systems (MAS) is still an open issue, especially in relation to integrated frameworks that consider the co-specification of their different dimensions. The development of MAS in JaCaMo [1] comprises three distinct dimensions, namely: agent, organisation, and environment. However, these dimensions are not uniformly integrated into a single formalism: agents are programmed in Jason [2] using the AgentSpeak language; organisations are specified in Moise [3] in an XML-based document; and environments are coded in Java using the CArtAgO API [4]. This approach makes difficult to keep track of problems because errors in one level can affect the other levels, and it also becomes cumbersome to explore interconnections between the different layers and requires the programmer the knowledge about different paradigms. To address these issues, we propose a unified representation which covers these three agent programming dimensions and integrates the various formalisms. Thus, we developed ontologies to represent the agency, environment, and organisation levels of MAS, which are aligned with a platform integrating these three

F. Koch et al. (Eds.): CARE/AVSA 2014, CCIS 498, pp. 22–33, 2015.

levels in agent programming (*i.e.*, JaCaMo [1]). Until now, JaCaMo platform does not address the ontological level of MAS. Hence, we discuss an integrated semantic model to represent these three dimensions based on ontologies that represent each MAS level.

In order to demonstrate the need for and advantages of an integrated view for knowledge representation when developing complex multi-agent systems, we show how our approach can be used to model a multi-agent assisted living application aiming at supporting home care for an elderly patient. In particular, we support the collaborative work of a team of people including family members and professional carers who work together to allow an elderly patient with various debilitating health conditions to live in his own home. We use multi-agent systems techniques and ambient intelligence to give such support, but beyond this, our vision is towards systems integration in smart cities through multi-agent systems techniques to allow full integration of data from city transport, health systems, social services, smart grids, and so forth. That is, we envision all such sources of information coming together to give as much support as possible to the patient's family and carers. This is a very important social scenario in Brazil where the predominant culture is for families to care for their elders themselves.

An integrated ontology model to represent these MAS dimensions enables semantic reasoning and can be used as a common vocabulary in agent-oriented programming. In our proposal these dimensions are sub-ontologies that may interconnect with each other, and reuse relevant concepts from each other MAS dimension. Each dimension details different aspects, and these interconnections when combined have to result in an integrated knowledge model with a clear correspondence to an integrated programming platform, such as JaCaMo [1]. Some proposals for the knowledge level, such as Moise [3], are already related to a programming framework, allowing to convert the ontology specification to a programming level [5]. This is desirable for all dimensions, but these levels have to be aligned for that to work as a common specification. Also, an MAS can be modelled, reused and extended in one dimension while maintaining the others, which allows the designer to work without going into specifics of the programming languages that define each dimension. In this context, an MAS design is more easily expressed and communicated, and the model can be more easily converted to a formal verification system. Thus, our work is a step towards a knowledge level integration of MAS dimensions and platforms.

This paper is structured as follows. Section 2 refers to previous ontologies related to MAS aspects: agents, organisations, and environments. Section 3 shows the need for the integration of such aspects at the knowledge level on the light of an example in the area of health care. Section 4 concludes this paper and points to our next steps.

2   Ontologies for Multi-Agent Systems

Agents are reactive systems that can independently determine how to best achieve their goals and perform their tasks [2] while demonstrating properties such as autonomy, reactivity, proactiveness and social ability. Agents are situated in an environment, where they can perceive and modify it, and they should be able to exchange information, cooperate and coordinate activities. Jason [2] is an AgentSpeak language platform implementation that focuses on agent actions and mental concepts. It is an open source interpreter that offers features such as speech-act based agent communication, plans annotation, architecture customisation, distributed execution and extensibility through internal actions. On the environment side of agent systems, CArtAgO [4] is a platform to support the artifact notion in MAS. Artifacts are function-oriented computational devices which provide services that agents can exploit to support their individual and social activities [4]. Lastly, the specification of agents at the organisation level can be achieved using an organisation modelling language, such as Moise [3]. Moise explicitly decomposes the specification of an organisation into its structural, functional and normative dimensions. Each of these three agent-oriented platforms addresses a specific dimension of MAS programming, and JaCaMo [1] integrates these three dimensions. Thus, an MAS programmed in JaCaMo is given by an agent organisation defined in Moise [3], organising autonomous agents coded in Jason [2], working in shared distributed artifact-based environments developed in CArtAgO [4]. In this paper, we are interested in the use of ontologies in these multi-agent platforms.

Ontologies are knowledge representation structures composed of concepts, relationships, instances and axioms, which empower the execution of semantic reasoners that provide functionalities such as *consistency checking*, *concept satisfiability*, *classification*, and *realisation*. It is natural to think that there are advantages in using ontologies more expressively in agent development. One of the first approaches to consider the use of ontologies to enhance agent-oriented programming was AgentSpeak-DL [6], which extended AgentSpeak with description logic concepts. However, their focus was on using ontologies during agent reasoning, instead of modelling aspects of MAS in ontologies. In other words, there are many ways in which these areas can be connected and explored in the literature; in fact, JaCaMo dimensions have been considered at the knowledge level in previous work, as done for instance in [5]. However a multi-dimensional unified view has not been proposed. The work in [6] points advantages of integrating agents and ontologies: (*i*) more expressive queries in the belief base, since results can be inferred from the ontology and thus are not limited to explicit knowledge; (*ii*) refined belief update given that ontological consistency of a belief addition can be checked; (*iii*) the search for a plan to deal with an event is more flexible because it is not limited to unification, *i.e.*, it is possible to consider subsumption relationships between concepts; and (*iv*) agents can share knowledge using ontology languages such as OWL (Web Ontology Language). Next we focus on some examples of ontologies proposed for MAS, specially considering the distinct dimensions which divide JaCaMo. Although the advantages of using ontologies for agents are clear, few agent-oriented platforms are currently integrated with ontology techniques.

2.1 Ontologies in Agent Programming and Reasoning

Considering the agent dimension, AgentSpeak-DL [6] is an agent-oriented programming language based on Description Logic (DL). AgentSpeak-DL extends agents' belief base with DL in which the belief base includes: (*i*) one immutable TBox (terminological box, or conceptualisation) that characterises the domain concepts and properties; and (*ii*) one ABox (assertion box, or instantiation) with dynamic factual knowledge that changes according to the results of environment perception, plan execution and agent communication. In this approach, the agent belief base can be enriched with the definition of complex concepts that can go beyond factual knowledge [6].

JASDL [7] followed these ideas to transparently merge agent belief base and ontological reasoning. JASDL [7] is an AgentSpeak-DL implementation that extended Jason to provide agents with ontology manipulation capabilities using the OWL API [7]. This offers a practical approach to agents use ontologies and semantic reasoning in declarative paradigms. Agent programmers benefit from features such as plan trigger generalisation based on ontological knowledge and the use of such knowledge in belief base querying [7]. Some Jason modules were altered to implement JASDL, *e.g.*, the belief base was extended to partly resides within an ontology ABox, which, combined with a DL reasoner, facilitates the reuse of available knowledge in ontologies. This feature increases the inferences that an agent can make based on its beliefs and assures knowledge consistency. JASDL [7] also modified Jason plan library to enable enhanced plan searching; and agent architecture to augment it with message processing to obtain semantically-enriched inter-agent communication.

This section presented approaches for incorporating ontological reasoning in agents to enable them to relate with knowledge and not only with the observation of facts. However, to the best of our knowledge, approaches for represent the agent dimension in ontologies concerning the Jason platform do not exist yet. Next section shows a knowledge representation of the environment dimension of MAS using ontologies.

2.2   Ontologies for Environments and Artifacts

Environments play an essential role in MAS, and their semantic representation can improve the way agents reason about the objects with which they interact and the overall environment where they are situated. In [8] an environment ontology is proposed based on environment aspects of agent programming technologies that is integrated into a platform for developing cognitive multi-agent simulations. Thus, it can be used to specify environments and derive a project-level, complete, and executable definition of multi-agent environments [8]. An environment description is a specification of its properties and behaviour, which includes concepts such as: *objects* (*i.e.*, resources of the environment); *agents* (*i.e.*, their "physical" representation in the environment that is visible to other agents); *actions* that each type of agent can perform in the environment; *reactions* of the environment and objects when an agent's actions affect them; *perception types* available to each type of agent; and *observable properties*, that is, the information about the simulation to which observers (*e.g.*, the agents) have access.

The use of an environment ontology adds three important features to existing multi-agent approaches [8]: *(i)* ontologies provide a common vocabulary to enable environment specification by agent developers (since an ontology explicitly represents a consensual model for environment and agent essential properties, defining environments in ontologies can facilitate and improve the development of multi-agent simulations); *(ii)* an environment ontology is useful for agents acting in the environment because it provides a common vocabulary for communication within and about the environment (such explicit conceptualisation is essential to allow interoperability of heterogeneous systems); and *(iii)* environment ontologies can be defined in ontology editors with graphical user interfaces, making easier for those unfamiliar with programming to understand and design such ontologies. In [8], the relationship between the environment and other MAS dimensions was already foreseen, since they mention the intention of looking at higher-level aspects of environments, *i.e.*, social environment aspects of agents, such as the specification of social norms and organisations in agent societies. Next section shows what has been proposed regarding the knowledge level of the social dimension.

2.3   Ontologies for Social Organisations

Agent organisations are required to provide the means for agents to query and reason about the structure of a society of agents [5]. Among the recent developments on Moise, there is already a semantic description of multi-agent organisations [5], using OWL to develop an ontology for organisational specifications of the Moise model (structural, functional, and normative levels). This approach may help agents in becoming aware, querying, and reasoning about their social and organisational context in a uniform way [5]. Also, this work makes possible to convert the ontology and the Moise specification, providing more flexibility for the development of agent organisations.

The semantic description of Moise [5] provides agent-side reasoning and querying features (*i.e.*, the agents are able to use this information). The benefits highlighted in [5] are increased modularisation, knowledge enriching with meta-data, reuse of specifications, and easier integration. With the semantic web effort aiming to represent the information in semantic formats, the MAS community can take advantage of new semantic technologies in MAS development tasks such as to integrate organisational models, to monitor organisations, and to analyse agent societies [5].

3   Unifying the Three Dimensions

For each of the three dimensions described above it would be interesting to establish semantic representations of their particular type of abstractions. For each of them the advantages of semantic web technologies have been advocated, and they usually recognise the importance of the other dimensions. However, a global view of MAS is still missing. We aim to work towards the integration of these various dimension at the semantic level, since they are already being integrated at the programming level (for example in JaCaMo [1]) and each dimension has had proposals for a semantic account.

Agent programmers benefit from an integration among these ontological levels with each programming dimension since the knowledge represented in one dimension can be reused in another, resulting in a greater interoperability of agent platforms. This would enable to convert MAS defined in ontologies to code in specific agent platforms, and vice-versa. Also, a system designed with a higher degree of modularity is easier to maintain, given that it separates different concerns yet enables relations between them. For example, the characteristics of one dimension (*e.g.*, environment) could be used to define properties on another (*e.g.*, organisational). In fact, it is often the case that the concepts of one level are related to another but current MAS platforms do not allow for such relations to be explicitly represented. The JaCaMo ontology is structured in a way that it imports three ontologies in order to represent: the agent dimension in Jason, the environment layer in CArtAgO, and the organization elements in Moise. This modularization separates different MAS concerns in independent components, while allowing to include and interrelate them, therefore offering advantages sush as increased manutenability, usability and extensibility for the MAS developers.

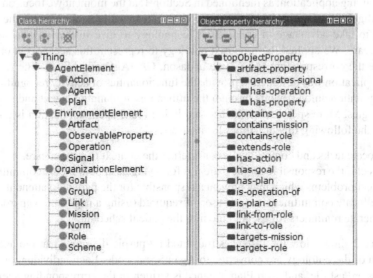

Fig. 1. Classes and object properties in our proposed JaCaMo ontology

More specifically, the classes and properties in the JaCaMo ontology we are proposing can be visualized in Figure 1, which shows an overview of the concepts in the dimensions modelled in three sub-ontologies: agent, environment and social organisation. Figure 1, obtained in the Protégé ontology editor[1], shows the concepts in yellow circles at left and the properties in blue rectangles at right. From the agent dimension, in Jason [2], the most important concepts are the agents, their plans and actions. From the CArtAgO [4] environment perspective, the main concepts are the artifacts, their operations, observable properties, and signals. Artifacts can be either the target (outcome) of agent activities, or the tools used by agents as means to support their activities (consequently, artifacts reduce the complexity of agents tasks' execution). Finally, the Moise [3] organisation elements are, for example, groups, roles, missions, norms, and so on. A role definition states that agents playing that role are willing to accept the behavioural constraints related to it. The organisation functional dimension specifies how global collective goals should be achieved, *i.e.*, how they are decomposed in global plans, grouped in coherent sets (missions) to be individually distributed to agents. The normative dimension binds the structural dimension with the functional one to specify role's permissions, prohibitions and obligations for missions [3]. The connections among concepts are encoded by means of the object properties, which determine how instances are allowed to relate among each other. Next we show how to use this ontology to model, reason and generate code for a JaCaMo ambient intelligence application that provides its users health care functionalities.

---

[1] Available open source at http://protege.stanford.edu/

3.1 Modelling a Health Care Application in the JaCaMo Ontology

The designed JaCaMo ontology was instantiated to model and generate a multi-agent assisted living application; as mentioned in Section 1, at the moment we focus on ambient intelligence and multi-agent systems to support team collaboration, but in the future we aim to take advantage of smart cities technology to give further support to family eldercare. We applied the proposed ontology to represent this scenario in order to generate the corresponding MAS code in Jason, CArtAgO and Moise. The resulting MAS application was designed to provide the functionalities of activity recognition and task negotiation among agents through the utilization of planning, agent and semantic technologies. More specifically, the assisted living multi-agent application is going to provide the following functionalities for its users:

1. Allocate tasks and commitments considering the context of patient care.
2. Detect if the responsible for the patient is following its appointments/commitments.
3. Detect problems which may prevent a responsible for the patient to attend its tasks.
4. Reallocate commitments among users if required (using a negotiation approach).
5. Generate reminders for users to monitor the patient schedule.

Figure 2 shows how the instances (depicted by purple diamonds) in the agent dimension of the ontology are converted to AgentSpeak code. Each individual of Agent becomes an .asl file, and each Plan instance is written in the corresponding agent file, which is retrieved according to the ontology properties (*e.g.*, **has-plan** and **is-plan-of**).

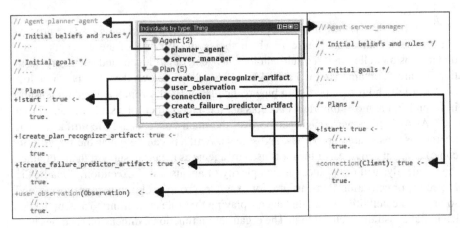

Fig. 2. Agent dimension instantiation in our ontology and generation of AgentSpeak code

The **planner_agent**, shown in Figure 2, is responsible for the heavy reasoning tasks such as plan recognition, failure prediction and plan negotiation and reallocation (in case of failure). The **planner_agent** extracts the relevant information (*e.g.*, specific sensor readings) from the received observation, and, with the extracted contextual information, it tries to recognize the plan that the user is executing using the Plan Recognizer component (the **SBRArtifact** explained later in this paper). After recognizing a plan, the **planner_agent** tries to predict if the plan is going to fail using the Failure Predictor component (implemented in the **FailurePredictorArtifact**, to be explained later).

If the agent can not determine which of the plans the user is executing (there is more than one candidate plan), the agent stops the recognition and waits for the next observation. After a new observation is received, the recognition process is resumed. The **server_manager** agent is responsible for setting the system initial infrastructure and for establishing and managing the connections between an interface agent and a planner agent. The interface agents are responsible for collecting sensor readings from the system related devices, such as the user smartphone, and send them to their respective planner agents as observations. However, the interface agent code lie outside the scope of the MAS project exemplified here. The connection of an interface agent is signalized through the event "+connection(Client)" in the **server_manager** agent, in which Client corresponds to the name (identification) of the connected agent.

Figure 3 shows how the instances in the environment dimension of the ontology are converted to CArtAgO code. Each instance of Artifact generates an .java file, and each Operation individual generates a Java method in the corresponding artifact file (according to the **has-operation** property). The integration of agents with artifacts, such as the Plan Recognizer and the Failure Predictor, is based on a set of CArtAgO and Jason agent language elements such as events and beliefs.

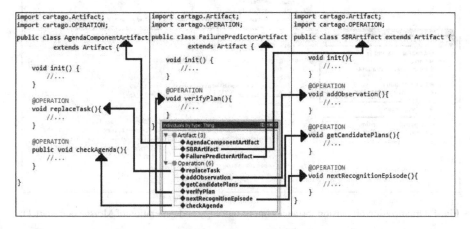

Fig. 3. Environment dimension instantiation in our ontology and generation of CArtAgO code

The **AgendaComponentArtifact** is used to store and manage commitments, thus it uses the operations **replaceTask** and **checkAgenda** to achieve this. The other artifact, named **FailurePredictorArtifact**, was designed to identify whether a plan is likely going to fail. To accomplish this, the **verifyPlan** operation tries to predict if the plan (correspondent to planID) is going to fail given the contextual information (context). The context parameter corresponds to the same list of predicates used to generate the observation in the Plan Recognizer example. The third and last artifact, called **SBRArtifact**, was developed to recognize plans by applying a symbolic approach which derives candidate plans according to a sequence of observations. To achieve this, the **addObservation** operation converts a set of binary predicates (received as a list of java objects) into an observation object that is used as input for the Symbolic Plan Recognition technique. The **getCandidatePlans** operation returns a list of candidate plans (determined based on the previous added observations). The returned list is included in the agent belief base as a predicate containing a list of plan names (identifications). The **nextRecognitionEpisode** operation stops the current recognition episode. When the recognition is stopped, all the information relating to the episode is erased (*e.g.*, observations counter).

Figures 4 and 5 show how the instances in the organization dimension of the ontology are converted to Moise code. The mapping is straightforward since individuals of concepts such as Role, Group, Mission and Norm are directly mapped to the XML Moise code. Figure 4 demonstrates the Moise structural specification for the assisted living application MAS scenario, which defines the following roles: patient, carer, family member, responsible for patient, adult family member and not adult family member. In this context, a group must be composed of at least one patient, one carer and one agent playing the role of responsible for the patient. Moreover, the links establish communication constraints, *e.g.*, agents playing the role of responsible for the patient have authority over carers (*i.e.*, they are allowed to send goals to be achieved by carer agents).

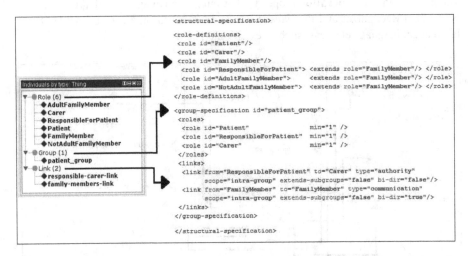

Fig. 4. Organization dimension instances in our ontology and generation of Moise code (part 1)

Figure 5 demonstrates the functional and normative specification of the Moise for the assisted living application. In this context, the carer is obligated through a norm to perform the mission of provide pills to the patient. Also, not adult family members are prohibited of executing the mission of proving physiotherapy to the patient. This specification also defines how the missions are decomposed in goals. For example, the mission to provide the patient physiotherapy requires to achieve the goals of prepare the patient, move to clinic and wait for patient.

The representation of MAS in ontologies provides not only the code generation functionality, but also reasoning features. Figure 6 exemplifies (through the Protégé interface) asserted object properties(*e.g.*, that the server_manager Agent has-plan connection) and inferred properties (*e.g.*, that the start Plan is-plan-of planner_agent).

Semantic reasoning allows to infer knowledge which is implicit derived from axioms explicit asserted in the ontology. Besides inferences, modelling an MAS in ontologies

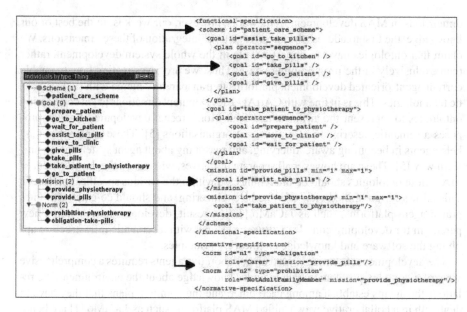

```
<functional-specification>
  <scheme id="patient_care_scheme">
    <goal id="assist_take_pills">
      <plan operator="sequence">
        <goal id="go_to_kitchen" />
        <goal id="take_pills" />
        <goal id="go_to_patient" />
        <goal id="give_pills" />
      </plan>
    </goal>
    <goal id="take_patient_to_physiotherapy">
      <plan operator="sequence">
        <goal id="prepare_patient" />
        <goal id="move_to_clinic" />
        <goal id="wait_for_patient" />
      </plan>
    </goal>
    <mission id="provide_pills" min="1" max="1">
      <goal id="assist_take_pills" />
    </mission>
    <mission id="provide_physiotherapy" min="1" max="1">
      <goal id="take_patient_to_physiotherapy"/>
    </mission>
  </scheme>
</functional-specification>

<normative-specification>
  <norm id="n1" type="obligation"
        role="Carer" mission="provide_pills"/>
  <norm id="n2" type="prohibition"
        role="NotAdultFamilyMember" mission="provide_physiotherapy"/>
</normative-specification>
```

Fig. 5. Organization dimension instances in our ontology and generation of Moise code (part 2)

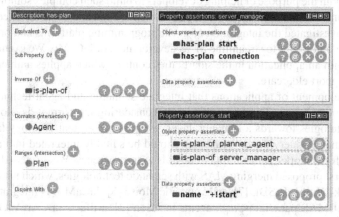

Fig. 6. Object properties asserted and inferred through the execution of semantic reasoning

offers the possibilities of enhancing how the developer design and visualize their Ja-CaMo projects. With this example, we intended to show the importance of the interrelation of these distinct levels, how complementary previous approaches are, and how crucial a unified view at the knowledge-level is for MAS development, which is being proposed by means of ontologies. Thus, this paper explores ways of integrating MAS with semantic technologies in the context of ambient intelligence applications.

4   Final Remarks

Integrating agent platforms with ontologies is expected to bring agents with the ability to operate in a Semantic Web context. We see efforts to integrate different programming dimensions in MAS development frameworks, however, our work is, to the best of our knowledge, the first to address the knowledge level integration of these dimensions. We claim that ontologies have an important role in the whole system development, rather than exclusively in the programming phase. Thus, we are investigating how to enable current agent-oriented development platforms to transparently merge with such semantic technologies. This is in line with CArtAgO development directions [4] in considering ontologies to represent the artifacts, and with Moise recent developments which proposes a semantic description of multi-agent organisations [5]. These approaches may help agents in becoming aware, querying, and reasoning about agent systems in an uniform way [5]. These are however all separate initiatives, whereas in the development of MAS these ontologies should be interconnected within the various specification levels. This allows for an unified view of systems engineering, and should co-exist with integrated agent platforms, such as JaCaMo [1]. As result, developers may obtain a new paradigm for developing complex software systems with a semantic infrastructure applying the software and knowledge engineering principles.

The development of services based on collaborative agents requires a comprehensive view of a complex problem, which includes knowledge about the environment, the relations the agents establish among each other, and the common plans that they have to deal with in a collaborative way. Unified MAS platforms such as JaCaMo [1] are being developed with the purpose of helping developers to build such complex solutions, however, such unification must happen during the system design and at the knowledge level. Thus, we investigated the integration of agent programming platforms and ontologies, by applying ontologies to streamline MAS development in JaCaMo. We exemplify our approach with an application in the smart cities context, which applies ambient intelligence to support eldercare.

The development of applications that integrate semantic and agent technologies is still an open challenge. To address this issue, considering the current development of agent technologies towards a semantic layer, we pointed out that ontology languages offering semantic querying and reasoning should be suitably integrated into agent development frameworks, for example in regards to transparency. We discussed previous work that first proposed merging MAS with semantic technologies, which is the case of AgentSpeak-DL [6], JASDL [7], and Semantic Moise [5]. JaCaMo [1] integrates different levels of MAS paradigms, e.g., agents in Jason [2], artifacts in CArtAgO [4], and organisations in Moise [3]. This work discussed the integration of these levels through ontologies. The inclusion of ontology technologies in MAS is expected to bring together the power of knowledge-rich approaches and complex distributed systems. In terms of MAS design, such an integrated approach allows the design of a global conceptual view, and semantic tools make it possible to verify model consistency, perform inferences using semantic reasoners, query instantiated models, develop and visualize MAS specifications in ontologies, all of which can contribute to a more principled way to develop multi-agent systems.

Acknowledgements. Part of the results presented in this paper were obtained through research on a project titled "Semantic and Multi-Agent Technologies for Group Interaction", sponsored by Samsung Eletrônica da Amazônia Ltda. under the terms of Brazilian federal law No. 8.248/91.

References

1. Boissier, O., Bordini, R.H., Hübner, J., Ricci, A., Santi, A.: Multi-agent oriented programming with JaCaMo. Science of Computer Programming 78(6), 747–761 (2013)
2. Bordini, R.H., Hübner, J.F., Wooldridge, M.: Programming multi-agent systems in AgentSpeak using Jason. John Wiley & Sons (2007)
3. Hübner, J.F., Boissier, O., Kitio, R., Ricci, A.: Instrumenting multi-agent organisations with organisational artifacts and agents. Autonomous Agents and Multi-Agent Systems 20(3), 369–400 (2010)
4. Ricci, A., Viroli, M., Omicini, A.: CArtAgO: An infrastructure for engineering computational environments in MAS. In: Weyns, D., Parunak, H.V.D., Michel, F. (eds.) 3rd International Workshop "Environments for Multi-Agent Systems" (E4MAS), pp. 102–119 (2006)
5. Zarafin, A.M.: Semantic description of multi-agent organizations. Master's thesis, Automatic Control and Computers Faculty, Computer Science and Engineering Department – University "Politehnica" of Bucharest (2012)
6. Moreira, Á.F., Vieira, R., Bordini, R.H., Hübner, J.F.: Agent-oriented programming with underlying ontological reasoning. In: Baldoni, M., Endriss, U., Omicini, A., Torroni, P. (eds.) DALT 2005. LNCS (LNAI), vol. 3904, pp. 155–170. Springer, Heidelberg (2006)
7. Klapiscak, T., Bordini, R.H.: JASDL: A practical programming approach combining agent and semantic web technologies. In: Baldoni, M., Son, T.C., van Riemsdijk, M.B., Winikoff, M. (eds.) DALT 2008. LNCS (LNAI), vol. 5397, pp. 91–110. Springer, Heidelberg (2009)
8. Okuyama, F.Y., Vieira, R., Bordini, R.H., da Rocha Costa, A.C.: An ontology for defining environments within multi-agent simulations. In: Workshop on Ontologies and Metamodeling in Software and Data Engineering (2006)

VIRTUAL-ME: A Library for Smart Autonomous Agents in Multiple Virtual Environments

Roberta Castano, Giada Dotto, Rossella Suma, Andrea Martina, and Andrea Bottino

Department of Control and Computer Engineering, Politecnico di Torino
Corso Duca degli Abruzzi, 24, 10129 Torino, Italy
{roberta.castano,giada.dotto,rossella.suma}@studenti.polito.it
{andrea.martina,andrea.bottino}@polito.it

Abstract. Emulating human behaviour is a very desirable characteristic for virtual agents. There is plenty of literature that focuses on a single specific aspect of human behaviour emulation, but it is quite rare to find a collection of implementations encompassing several aspects of the problem. In this work we present VIRTUAL-ME (VIRTUal Agent Library for Multiple Environments), a library that provides programmers with a complete set of classes that assembles various human characteristics and makes it possible to build smart agents. The assessment of the library capabilities to populate a generic virtual environment is also discussed through the analysis of different case studies.

Keywords: Autonomous Virtual Human, Intelligent Virtual Agents, Interactive Virtual Environments.

1 Introduction

Artificial intelligence (AI) has received increasing attention over the last thirty years. It has been used successfully in many fields such as finance, medicine, games, robotics and the web. In particular, in recent years, a quite complex area of research has emerged: the simulation of the autonomous behaviour of characters in computer graphics. More than any other field in AI, this one requires careful investigation into human behaviour and cognitive psychology in order to be able to model and reproduce accurate simulations. Over the last three decades, scientists have attempted to model all kinds of human behaviour, using simulation and visualization, primarily aimed at creating educational and training systems. Nevertheless, human behaviour simulation is also widely used in programs with entertainment, commercial and non-educational purposes. A large variety of applications adopt some kind of human behaviour emulation, from crowd control and evacuation planning to traffic density and safety [13].

The general problem of simulating (or creating) intelligence has been broken down into a number of specific sub-problems [11]. It is very common to find in the literature articles focusing on particular traits or capabilities desirable in an intelligent system. Investigations in the following fields appear to be the most popular: affective computing, emulation of human needs mechanism, environment perception, autonomous navigation of a virtual environment, memory models, event management and the overall agent behaviour mechanisms.

F. Koch et al. (Eds.): CARE/AVSA 2014, CCIS 498, pp. 34–45, 2015.

Emotions are a fundamental trait of human personality. In human science, emotions are often classified according to two main viewpoints. The first treats emotions as discrete constructs (an emotion is completely individual), while the second characterize them on a dimensional basis (an emotion is composed of interacting elementary components, [9]). Emotions can have different roles in driving agent behaviour, for example they can be used to select the next action or to control memory [12]. Researchers agree that the choice between basic or dimensional emotions - and which specific emotion within this category - should be based on the primary function of the agent and on the specific purposes of the application. In other words, it is not possible to elaborate a model capable of approaching every situation and environment, but it is reasonable to develop a model that can cover as many roles as possible.

An alternative way to drive an artificial agent is needs-based AI, where the next action picked is based on the agent's internal state and on the environmental inputs. Need fulfilment have been used, for instance, by Terzopoulos, to drive virtual pedestrians' behaviour [15], and in *The Sims* game [19]. Another possible mechanism is to define the agent behaviours in terms of responses to events ([14]).

Other researchers have been focusing on the problem of enabling the AI component to perceive and explore its environment. For example, Tu described a framework to simulate artificial fish in which the perception relied on a visual sensor spanning a 300-degree angle around the fish head ([17]).

In addition to a vision system, a smart agent should be equipped with a navigation system, whose purpose is to provide a path without obstacles from one point to another in the environment. This task is usually broken down in two subtasks: global navigation, which uses a pre-learned map of the space, and local navigation, providing the ability to avoid unexpected obstacles along the path relying on the agent sensory system. The majority of researchers, faced the problem of navigation adopting a central collision avoidance system that controls the agents' movements.

The agent's capability to influence the environment is defined by a set of possible actions that reflects on changes to the state of the environment itself. All actions that humans undertake in an environment are influenced by their emotional and physical state and by their personality. To create believable virtual characters, these factors must be taken into account. This makes the creation of agents emulating the rich complexity of humans a real challenge.

Among the possible behaviour management models, several researchers recommend the use of the *Behaviour Trees* (BTs). The Behaviour Tree is a "simple data structure that provides graphical representation and formalisation for complex actions" [6]. The first implementation of BTs appeared in 2004 in a one-act interactive drama called Façade, and since then, they have been increasingly used by game AI programmers to create more exciting and complex characters. Their effectiveness is witnessed by the fact that important games, like Spore (in 2007), Halo3 (in 2008), and NBA '09, adopted this approach.

The contribution of VIRTUAL-ME is the capability to deal with different aspects related to the management of autonomous characters behaving like humans. Based on the analysis of the peculiarity of these aspects, this work proposes an organic, all-encompassing and real-time solution that can facilitate programmers and scientists in populating a virtual environment with a crowd of smart agents. This library enables the creation of different worlds populated with several independent agents, incorporating general cases that bring together most human behaviours and that can be easily extended to deal with other peculiar cases.

The rest of the paper is organized as follows. Section 2 describes the different elements concurring to define the behaviour of the autonomous agents and discusses their integration. Section 3 presents some experiments aimed at assessing the effectiveness of the library. Finally, Section 4 concludes the paper and outlines future works.

2   The VIRTUAL-ME Library

The VIRTUAL-ME library was created after an in-depth analysis of the state of the art of various fields and proposes solutions to deal with the following key issues:

- agent behaviour mechanisms;
- affective computing;
- the emulation of human needs mechanism;
- the environment perception problem, especially the vision;
- the problem of navigating a virtual environment;
- memory models;
- event management.

All these elements, detailed in the following sub-sections, concur to compose a reproduction as accurate as possible of human intelligence. In the library, the virtual human management is implemented by a Behaviour Tree (BT). The accomplishment of the chosen actions is dictated by a combination of both needs and emotion emulation techniques and characters have been equipped with a perception mechanism and the capability to explore the environment to fulfil their goals.

2.1   Affective Computing

An emotion is defined as a complex, subjective experience coupled with biological and behavioural changes. Emotions are capable of altering attention, or the likelihood of a certain behavioural response, activating associative memories, influencing the learning process and aiding social behaviour [5]. Defining emotional states appropriately can determine a more accurate representation of human behaviour.

While most models are tailored to a specific scenario, the solution implemented in our work offers a generic emotion model designed to be a good compromise between simplicity and granularity (in terms of emotion description).

The model conceived in this project was inspired by the work of Thayer [3] and Russell [10]. It is controlled by two dimensions: *Activity* and *Mood* (see Figure 1). Low values of the Activity parameter represent a more phlegmatic attitude, whereas high values identify a hyperactive disposition. For example, in some people, a negative event can induce a despairing reaction, with a sense of paralysis, while in other people it can rouse a furious reaction. The Mood parameter, on the other hand, identifies a negative valence with low values, while a positive value identifies a pleasant demeanour. As an example, in an emergency situation some people's reaction is negative, driving them to despair and other people might remain serene and in control.

To create a more varied and heterogeneous (*i.e.* a more believable) collection of agents, each of them is created with a basic personal attitude that is chosen randomly. Then, the agent emotions is modified by the interaction with other agents or with the environment. Once a change has occurred, the agent will return to his primal emotion after a period of time.

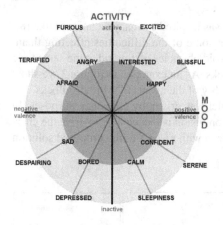

Fig. 1. Emotion Representation

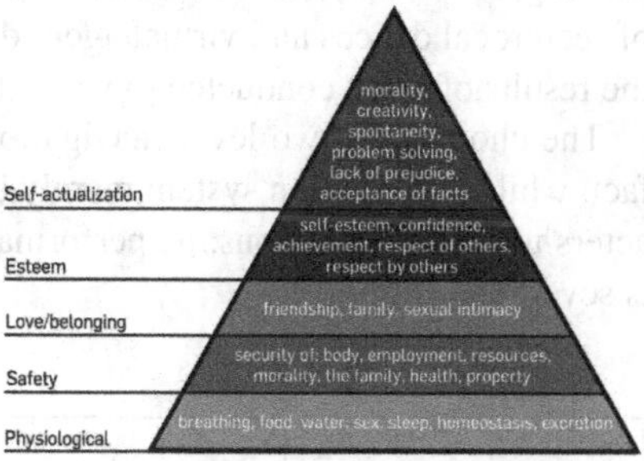

Fig. 2. Maslow needs hierarchy pyramid

2.2 Emulation of Human Needs

The implementation of needs is one of the most common techniques used in video games to drive autonomous agents. In this frame, an agent has a set of ever-changing needs that demand to be satisfied. To this end, the agent figures out what can be done on the basis of what is available in the surrounding environments. Inside the library, the application designer can define, for each type of agents, a specific set of needs, their domains and how they would evolve.

In our test cases we modeled human needs according to the model proposed by the psychologist Abraham Maslow [7]. He suggested that people are motivated to first fulfill basic needs before moving on to more advanced needs (Figure 2). Thus, in our examples, we considered most of the basic needs (like hunger, thirst or physiological needs) and some of the higher level needs (such as friendship and self-preservation) described by Maslow.

2.3 Navigation

The VIRTUAL-ME Library implements a "decentralized" navigation system that allows the agents to be autonomous in their choices. A two levels navigation model was designed. The first level manages the global navigation problem relying on the A* algorithm [2]. A* requires to map the walkable area with a graph, which can be done only when obstacles are known *a priori*. Thus, the second level is responsible of handling dynamic obstacles, such as moving objects, agents or new hurdles created during the simulation. Agents have been equipped with a visual system that provides the ability to perceive the environment: an object is "seen" if at least one of its vertices falls into the agent's field of view and its vertices are not occluded by another object. If a potential collision is detected by the vision system, a force is applied to the agent to change the direction and speed of its motion. Summarizing, while A* determines the main path as a sequence of nodes, vision allows agents to walk from one node to another avoiding unexpected obstacles.

The design of our local navigation system was inspired by many techniques like [8], [1] and [18] and improved in order to correct some of the difficulties affecting them, proving, for instance, to be able to properly avoid obstacles getting rid at the same time of reciprocal dances and virtual agent deadlocks. As an example, in Figure 3 we show the results of a test conducted to verify the ability of the agents to avoid deadlocks.

The choice of a two levels navigation model was driven by efficiency purposes. In fact, while a navigation system merely based on vision is indeed able to drive the characters to their destinations, its performance drop with respect to the proposed solution is severe (see Figure 4).

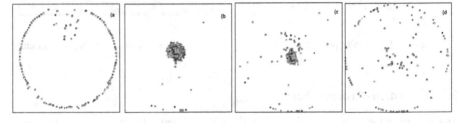

Fig. 3. Example of deadlock avoidance: (a) 120 agents on a circle are instructed to reach their antipodal position; (b) a congestion forms in the middle of the circle but (c-d) it is quickly resolved

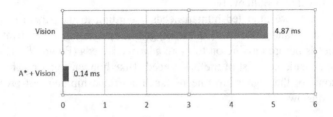

Fig. 4. Comparison of the average per frame computational times of the two levels and of the vision-based only navigation systems in a reference environment (the Casino described in Section 3)

2.4 Memory Model

Memory is an element that allows the agent to remember past information and to learn from past experiences. Considering this element to drive the agent behaviour is relevant, as the lack of a storage mechanism could lead to mistakes or damaging repeated behaviours which would make agents appear less believable.

Our current implementation considers a very simplistic model, which stores a FIFO list of the agents or objects the agent interacted with and, for each of them, a piece of information summarizing the changes in the agent emotion determined by this interaction. In order to simulate the human process of forgetting information, the lists have a constant length and items are removed after a certain time.

2.5 Events

An event is an occurrence that takes place in a virtual world. It is caused by environmental factors or agents' actions.

In VIRTUAL-ME, an *event generator* starts and ends the events and eventually makes them evolve in time. Each agent can be associated with an *event responder*, which contains all possible actions that the agent can do, according to his personality and to the event urgency (or priority), when a specific event is notified.

The event managing mechanism will be further discussed in the next paragraph due to its interconnection with the agent behaviour. A detailed example will be also discussed in section 3.1.

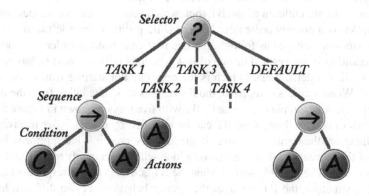

Fig. 5. An example of Behaviour Tree

2.6 Interactions with the Surrounding World

As a final element influencing the agent behaviour, we took into consideration the agent interactions with the surrounding environment. To model these interactions, both the environment and the objects or agents it contains can expose different attributes. These attributes are defined in an XML file associated to each category of objects and an agent can query them. The retrieved information can then be used to make decisions or to control the agent actions. For example if an agent is willing to gamble, it will look for a gamble table that has a croupier and free seats. When such a table has been found, the agent can walk towards the location of a free seat.

2.7 Agent Behaviour

As described in the previous sections, the demeanour of our virtual humans is determined by their emotions, needs and memory (*i.e.*, their internal state) and by the state of the environment (*i.e.*, their external state). Furthermore, agents have the ability to navigate through the environment, interact with it and with the objects it includes and to respond to events.

In order to manage all these elements, the agents' behaviour has been implemented using Behaviour Trees (BT). A BT defines and manages agents' *tasks*, which are related to the fulfilment of their needs and to their reaction to events.

In the BT, an agent task is represented by a sub-tree whose root has an ordered set of child nodes, which are leaves of the BT. When a task is activated, the leaves are executed one by one in order from left to right. The first child of the task is always a *Condition* node that tests the agent's internal state and the external state to check if the agent wants to or can realize the specific task. If the condition is verified, the task execution is broken down into a set of sub-tasks managed by *action* nodes. An active action node has one of the following three states: *Success* (the leaf has been completed correctly); *Running* (the action will continue during the next simulation step); *Failed* (the leaf has ended incorrectly). A task is successful only if all of its children succeed, otherwise, it reflects the state of the current active child.

All agent tasks are children of the BT root, which acts as a selector, sequencing the different tasks on a priority order based on the child position (from left to right). The agent behaviour is managed as follows: the tree root calls tasks in order of priority. If the task condition is not verified or one of task's actions fails, the next task is started. If all tasks fail, the default task (which is the only one not starting with a condition) is executed. When a task is completed, the BT restarts task scheduling from the one at highest priority. An example of an agent's BT with five tasks is shown in Figure 5.

The standard control flow of the BT can be modified by events. After receiving an event notification, the event response is immediately served if it has a priority higher than that of the current task being executed which will consequently terminate. Otherwise, the event will be possibly served when the BT activates the corresponding task.

With this structure, the BT manages the agent's behaviour at two different levels: a higher level that includes needs, emotions and memory; and a lower level formed by the agent's motion ability and perception system. The high level plans the agent's future actions, while the low level manages the way the agent reach physically its goal (path finding and object avoidance).

3 Results

VIRTUAL-ME Library has been implemented in C# and integrated into the Unity game engine (Unity Technologies, 2013). Simulations were carried out to test and explore the potentiality and effectiveness of the library. The two following environments were used.

Environment 1: The Casino. A virtual reconstruction of The Sands Hotel in the 60's, one of the most prestigious and oldest resort casinos in Las Vegas, which was entirely reconstructed in 3D for a previous Virtual Heritage project (Figure 6). Two of its main spaces were used for the simulations: the *Gamble room* with the gambling tables and the bar lounge, and the *Copa Room* where shows were performed every night. The Casino is a complex scenario consisting of more than 3.7M vertices.

Different types of agents were populating the environment: customers, barmen, waiters, croupiers and artists. Customers have by far the most complex behaviour. Besides managing events and satisfying basic internal needs (eating, drinking, resting or going to the toilet) they can also enjoy their time at the casino by playing and gambling, attending shows and interacting and speaking with other customers or casino personnel. Barmen and croupiers join their working place when there are customers to be served and interact with them according to customers' requests. Waiters manage table occupancies, customers orders and item delivery.

Two main events were scheduled in the simulation: a show in the Copa Room that agents can freely choose to attend, and an emergency situation, where each agent has to reach the nearest emergency exit.

Fig. 6. An image of the casino simulation

Environment 2: The Park. This environment depicts a park with a lake and other facilities, such as benches to rest, news-stands, a running path and some street food shops (Figure 7). A one way road and two pedestrian crossing were inserted, enabling agents to cross the road forcing the cars to stop. The agent types in this simulation are only two: drivers and pedestrians. The drivers have only a default task, which is driving across the park and stopping if any pedestrian crosses the road. Pedestrians behaviour include different tasks, such as eating, drinking, resting, running, watching the lake or buy a newspaper and read it. No events were registered for this environment. The number of vertices is 0.24M, far below those of the Casino.

3.1 Agent Behaviour Analysis

Although it is difficult to analyse all the details of the simulations, especially when the number of agents becomes very large, our observations allow us to state that in all the simulations the agents behaved as expected, acting according to their internal state and reacting properly to events.

Fig. 7. An image of the park simulation

Some examples observed in the Casino environment are the following. When the thirst level is high, agents reach the bar, or call a waiter if seated at a table, to place an order. When an agent is in a good mood, he has money to buy fiches and he is willing to play, he reaches a gambling table. The amount of time he spends playing depends on the game evolution. Wins and losses can change the agent emotional state, affecting his will to stay longer. Effective interactions between agents have been also observed when an agent wants to start a conversation. First, he looks for a potential partner, and if the counterpart agrees to have a chat, the conversation begins. According to the dialogue evolution, which was randomly selected among a set of possible options, the current emotions of the two agents can change.

Agents' response to events was also working as expected. Attending the show was a medium priority task. Thus, agents executing tasks at higher priority (such as having dinner at the tables) did not respond to the event until they completed their current tasks, while agents involved in tasks with the same priority of the show (e.g. gambling) were equally deciding to attend the show or continuing their activities. When the emergency event was triggered, given that this event has the highest priority among all tasks, all the agents rapidly left the casino through the nearest exit door (Figure 8).

3.2   Performance Analysis

We ran two simulations in each environment using different representations of the virtual humans. In the first case, referred to as *Humans*, the avatars were represented with a complete mesh, having an average resolution of 3.000 vertices, and avatars were animated with Motion Capture data. In the second case, referred to as *Capsules*, avatars were represented with an inanimate capsule (400 vertices). This choices aimed at separating the complexity of AI management from that of the agent graphical representation.

All simulations were run on a 64-bit intel core i5-2410M 2.3 GHz architecture with 6 GB of RAM and an NVIDIA Ge-Force GT 540M graphics card. The simulation results are summarized in Table 1.

The first tests were aimed at understanding how many agents could be managed in different simulation scenarios. To this end, we ran the simulation keeping on adding agents, until the frame rate dropped below 10 FPS. The Humans simulations could handle up to 130 agents for the park environment and 70 for the Casino, which, given the complexity of the environment and of the behaviour of its agents, can be considered

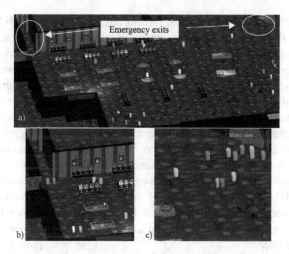

Fig. 8. (a) the agents in the casino before the emergency alert, (b-c) the agents evacuating the building through their closest emergency exit

Table 1. Overview of the performance results: maximal agent number (first column); execution time (in ms and FPS) for 50 agents (CPU column); computational resources per frame (in ms and percentage of execution time) required by VIRTUAL-ME (LIB column); total (CPU) and library functions (LIB) execution time per agent (Time/agent column); average amount of memory allocated per agent (Memory/agent column)

		Max number of agents	CPU (ms)	(FPS)	LIB (ms)	%	Time/agent CPU	LIB	Memory/agent (MB)
Casino	Hum	70	14.86	67.3	6.2	41.7	0.29	0.122	1.38
	Caps	95	11.20	89.3	5.4	48.2	0.21	0.106	0.58
Park	Hum	130	11.26	88.8	4.2	37.3	0.18	0.071	0.94
	Caps	250	11.17	89.5	4.0	35.8	0.17	0.067	0.42

as a reasonable result. The Capsules simulations reached up to 95 and 250 avatars for, respectively, the Casino and the park, showing that reducing the level of details of the avatar models results in a major increase of the library performances, especially in the park, where the agents have a less complex behaviour.

Further tests were aimed at collecting values of the resources used by the library. To this end, we ran each simulation with 50 agents profiling the application. Both Humans and Capsules simulations ran at real-time, with a worst case of 14.86 ms (67.3 FPS) for the Humans Casino. The library functions use a percentage of the CPU time between 36% and 48% in different cases. The estimated costs per agent shown in Table 1, obtained as the average CPU and library times per agent, provide an indication of the increase of the computational burden related to the population growth. The average memory allocated per agent ranges between 0.42 and 1.38 MB in the different simulations.

Comparison with Other Approaches. A thorough comparison with the many approaches to agent's behaviour management is virtually impossible. First, standardized reference benchmarks in this area are still missing or have not been widely acknowledged ([4]). Second, while VIRTUAL-ME provides a compromise between believability, autonomy and performances to manage real-time simulations, several approaches pursue different objectives, such as managing large crowds, usually simplifying the AI and adopting centralized solutions, or providing more complex behaviour mechanisms, which however often hamper the management of large number of agents.

The two approaches most similar to our research, in terms of agent complexity and number, are the work of Terzopoulos [15] and the RAIN library [16]. As for the first work, the maximal number of autonomous agents that can be handled in real time is approximately 100. To obtain a measure of merit on the RAIN library, we re-created the park environment and the same agent behaviours we used in our tests and kept on adding agents to the simulation, finding as 120 their limit number to maintain an interactive frame rate.

Concluding, though more complex tests in more challenging environments are required, our results suggests that VIRTUAL-ME is a valuable solution for the implementation and management of a quite large population of different types of smart agents, each with its own peculiar behaviour.

4   Conclusions

The emulation of the human behaviour is a difficult task that requires to face many different issues, which in the literature have been often addressed individually. In this paper, we described a system capable of combining and integrating the solution of many of the problems related to the management of autonomous human-like agents, such as: the development of a navigation system capable of handling both static and dynamic objects, the characterization of agents by means of an original affective model enriched with an emulation of human needs mechanism, the ability to respond to external events and the introduction of a memory model which helps agents to adapt to, and to learn from, the environment they "live" in.

The result of our research is VIRTUAL-ME, a software library that takes into account many human capabilities and characteristics. The library is highly flexible and can be easily adapted to different environments and used to depict many different kinds of agents. Our experimental tests have shown the good potentialities of the library.

Despite that, some of the library features are actually implemented according to simplistic models. Future work could involve providing more complex implementations of these functionalities. As an example, the memory model can be expanded in order to allow agents to "store" more complex information to enhance the learning process. Furthermore, in order to improve the usability of the library and to simplify its management for non skilled users, it would be useful and desirable to implement a graphical interface to help defining the agent behaviours.

References

1. Fiorini, P., Shillert, Z.: Motion planning in dynamic environments using velocity obstacles. International Journal of Robotics Research 17, 760–772 (1998)
2. Granberg, A.: A* pathfinding project (2013), http://arongranberg.com/astar/
3. Byeong, J.H., Seungmin, R., Sanghoon, J., Eenjun, H.: Music emotion classification and context-based music recommendation. Multimedia Tools Appl. 47(3), 433–460 (2010)
4. Kleiner, A., Farinelli, A., Ramchurn, S., Shi, B., Maffioletti, F., Reffato, R.: Rmasbench: Benchmarking dynamic multi-agent coordination in urban search and rescue (extended abstract). In: Proceedings of AAMAS 2013, pp. 1195–1196 (2013)
5. Levenson, R.: Human emotion: A functional view. Oxford Univarsity Press (1994)
6. Markowitz, D., Kider Jr., J.T., Shoulson, A., Badler, N.I.: Intelligent camera control using behavior trees. In: Allbeck, J.M., Faloutsos, P. (eds.) MIG 2011. LNCS, vol. 7060, pp. 156–167. Springer, Heidelberg (2011)
7. Maslow, A.H.: A theory of human motivation. Psychological Review 50, 370–396 (1943)
8. Reynolds, C.W.: Flocks, herds, and schools: A distributed behavioral model, pp. 25–34 (1987)
9. Rumbell, T., Barnden, J., Denham, S., Wennekers, T.: Emotions in autonomous agents: Comparative analysis of mechanisms and functions. Autonomous Agents and Multi-Agent Systems 25(1), 1–45 (2012)
10. Russell, J.A.: A circumplex model of affect. Journal of Personality and Social Psychology 39(6), 1161–1178 (1980)
11. Russell, S.J., Norvig, P.: Artificial Intelligence - A Modern Approach, 3rd edn. Pearson Education (2010)
12. Sceutz, M.: Useful roles of emotion in artificial agents: A case study from artificial life. In: Proceedings of the National Conference on Artificial Intelligence, pp. 42–48. MIT Press (2004)
13. Sharma, S., Otunba, S., Han, J.: Crowd simulation in emergency aircraft evacuation using virtual reality. In: 2012 17th International Conference on Computer Games (CGAMES), pp. 12–17 (2011)
14. Stocker, C., Sun, L., Huang, P., Qin, W., Allbeck, J.M., Badler, N.I.: Smart events and primed agents. In: Allbeck, J., Badler, N., Bickmore, T., Pelachaud, C., Safonova, A. (eds.) IVA 2010. LNCS (LNAI), vol. 6356, pp. 15–27. Springer, Heidelberg (2010)
15. Terzopoulos, D.: A reality emulator featuring autonomous virtual pedestrians and its application to distributed visual surveillance. In: Proc. IEEE Virtual Reality, pp. 1–4 (2008)
16. Rivel Theory. Rain
17. Tu, X., Terzopoulos, D.: Artificial fishes: Physics, locomotion, perception, behavior. J-COMP-GRAPHICS (Annual Conference Series) 28, 43–50 (1994)
18. van den Berg, J., Lin, M.C., Manocha, D.: Reciprocal velocity obstacles for real-time multi-agent navigation, pp. 1928–1935 (2008)
19. Will Wright. The sims code (1997), http://www.donhopkins.com/home/images/Sims/

Shared Message Boards for Smart Enterprises

Kelly Shigeno[1,3], Carlos Cardonha[3], Nicole Sultanum[3], Rodrigo L. Guimarães[3],
Mateus Molinaro[2,3], Ricardo Herrmann[3], Sergio Borger[3], and Fernando Koch[4]

[1] Faculdade de Arquitetura e Urbanismo - USP
kshigeno@usp.br
[2] Instituto de Pesquisas Tecnologicas
[3] IBM Research
[4] SAMSUNG Research Institute

Abstract. Shared Message Boards foster communication practices within restricted groups that typically do not emerge in traditional social networks. In this
article, we describe an experiment in which a Shared Message Board technology
was employed to support carpooling activities in a large company in Brazil. Based
on the results extracted from the platform and from two user studies, we identified
important elements influencing the adoption of this technology as well as other
activities where it can be effectively used in order to promote the development of
smart enterprises.

1 Introduction

Nowadays, it is possible to observe the existence of a large number of technologies supporting group communication. In particular, general-purpose solutions such as WhatsApp, Google Hangouts, Twitter, Facebook, and Google+ became so popular that they
are used in virtually every communication-oriented activity. However, there are scenarios for which privacy and context-based features provided by these application are still
unsatisfactory. Simultaneously, there is an increasing demand for highly personalized
tools (such as Google Now) which are heavily dependent on contextually rich data.

This setting motivates the investigation of community-oriented tools, since applications tailored for restrict groups are more prone to adoption and able to nurture the
emergence of special kinds of communication elements within the target audience. Consequently, they have the potential to generate context-specific data that cannot be easily
extracted from general-purpose social networks. Another important research question
consists of the identification of use cases where such tools could be more easily adopted.

Previously, we presented a Shared Message Board technology tailored for low-
income communities [18]. In this work, we report the experiences we had with this
application tailored as a carpooling tool for employees of a large company in Brazil. A
qualitative field research showed that this topic was not appealing for the target audience, and a quantitative survey was conducted to support the identification of topics for
which this technology can be more successfully applied.

This article is structured as follows. In Section 2 we present practical motivations for
this research and discuss related work. Section 3 describes the Shared Message Board
technology used in the experiment. Section 4 describes our carpooling case study as

F. Koch et al. (Eds.): CARE/AVSA 2014, CCIS 498, pp. 46–55, 2015.

well as follow-up qualitative and quantitative studies. We discuss lessons learned on Section 5 and finally conclude with potential directions for future work in Section 6.

2 Motivation and Related Work

This work is part of an extended research effort to investigate how computer-mediated communication tools can be employed in the enterprise. Namely, we are interested in understanding how individuals can use this technology to collaborate and socialize more effectively, and in providing better support to context-specific group tasks in the work-place.

Our research builds on previous findings in social media for local communities. In particular, this work was initially influenced by the Community Resource Messenger [15], a platform that has been implemented and deployed at shelters for homeless individuals. In another relevant effort, a system called Mobicomics [16] enabled people to create content for panels displayed in public locations using mobile phones. An important finding was that the solution fostered collaborative activities although it was not primarily designed for that.

Some articles have focused on the exploration of digital board applications on public displays. Brignall and Rogers [10] investigated challenges on the adoption of shared message boards. The authors indicated that a big barrier for citizen engagement with public displays is social embarrassment, and based on practical experiments they proposed models of interaction with such systems. Panorama [20] was created as a public display system designed to foster playfully-mediated social awareness of staff members in a department, and presents information about the environment like pictures on a virtual gallery. The Notification Collage [13] allows for co-located and distributed members of a community to publish media elements (*e.g.* pictures, videos and sticky notes) on a shared virtual board accessible on both public and personal displays.

Other interesting articles have addressed the use of text messaging for group communication. Battestini *et al.* [4] performed a large scale study on the use of text messages by teenager students in the United States. Their results indicated that students communicate with a large number of contacts for extended periods of time, engage in simultaneous conversations with many contacts, and often use text messaging as a method to switch between a variety of communication mediums. More recently, Church and Oliveira [11] investigated the motives and perceptions of using the WhatsApp mobile messaging application compared to traditional SMS. They found that while WhatsApp offers benefits such as cost, sense of community, and immediacy, SMS was still considered a more reliable, privacy preserving technology for mobile communication.

Finally, a large body of research has been dedicated to study the use of different communication tools – email, blogs, wikis, microblogging, social networks etc. – in the modern workplace ([3], [14], [19], [21]). In this work we go a step further by not just assessing existing communication tools but also reporting on the use of a shared message board implementation in a company over a 5-month period.

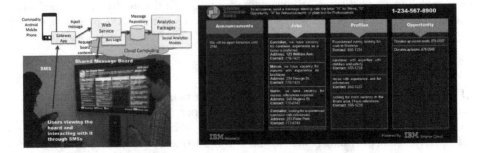

Fig. 1. On the left, an example of interaction with the Shared Message Board; on the right, a Shared Message Board interface customized for a job-seeking scenario

3 The Shared Message Board

In [18], we introduced a Shared Message Board tool whose main goal was to support ethnographic studies involving groups of people with disabilities in Brazil. The main conceptual goals guiding its design were the following: (i) enable easy technology absorption; (ii) incite meaningful social interactions; and (iii) facilitate the engagement community members. Since the proportion of individuals with difficulties to deal with technology within these groups is relatively large, this technology was designed to be easy to deploy and to allow for SMS-based user interaction. In this article, we discuss the application of this tool to the enterprise environment.

The Shared Message Board is a web-based tool whose goal is to foment community communication in the form of a digital board to be placed in open areas where it can be visualized by the target audience. It is embodied as a physical display, running a *public panel* specially tailored for that community; the interface design was conceived for Smart TVs due to their popularity and large screen space, but it is also suitable for traditional desktop monitors.

A public panel comprises a list of topics organised as *columns* (up to 4). Each column contain *messages* – contributions from community members – which are automatically refreshed with a slow scroll down animation to display all content. Messages are sent to the system through SMS, submitted to an unique phone number associated to this public panel. Users can choose which column to post on by adding an *identification character* (see example in Figure 1) in the beginning of the SMS message; a "default" column collects the messages without valid identification characters. Finally, the platform also provides a *user notification functionality* that can be used to inform contributors about new content relevant for them.

The system modules further include the *management portal*, the *gateway*, and the *back-end services*. The management portal allows for system administrators to fully configure and tailor boards to target communities, encompassing functions such as message filtering, user white/black-listing (determining which phone numbers can or cannot post), visual/content customization (*e.g.*, titles and icons), message aging (the "lifetime" of a message before it disappears), and column moderation flag (whether messages should be approved before being displayed). The gateway is a lightweight

Android app that intercepts each SMS message sent by users to the platform and injects it on the platform's back-end through HTTP over WiFi. Moreover, the gateway periodically polls the web server in order to verify if there are notifications to be forwarded to users (again, via SMS). Lastly, the back-end is a Java system that provides RESTful services to the gateway application, the public board's web interface, and the management portal, besides maintaining all database operations.

Our platform can be delivered as a cloud service, but cheap alternatives are also possible. In our experiment, we deployed the main services on a minimally equipped Raspberry Pi and the performance was satisfactory, showing that the system configuration and installation is simple and relatively cheap.

4 Case Study

We conducted an experiment by placing a Shared Message Board in the cafeteria of a large company in Brazil (see Figure 1). Initially, it was configured with the following four columns: **News** ("Notícias"), **Ride Offers** ("Ofereço Carona"), **Ride Requests** ("Busco Carona"), and **Open Forum** ("Fala, IBMista!"). Each column was associated to a key character ('n', 'o', 'b', and 'f', respectively), and messages that did not use them were posted in the open forum column. After a couple of months, the News column was substituted for **Classifieds** ("Classificados"), through which users could advertise things to sell or trade.

This initiative sought to promote interaction between the corporation's employees, to provide a new channel through which they could publicly express their opinions and feelings, and, more important, to facilitate the identification of potential carpooling partners. For this last feature, the back-end service was enriched with a *matchmaking logic* that takes carpooling request messages and tries to identify potential matching offers by checking co-occurrence of names indicating locations (marked by hashtags in the messages).

A relatively large number of messages were posted over the first weeks (specially in a day where a storm took place in the city), but then we observed a significant reduction in usage. Namely, the columns associated with the carpooling functionality received very few messages after the first two weeks. In order to understand why the adoption of our tool was so low, we decided to perform a qualitative approach, through which we tried to identify the profile of potential users, assess their experience with the Board, and verify what could motivate the tool's use.

4.1 Qualitative Approach

We employed two main methodologies for qualitative data collection: user observation and contextual inquiry interviews [8]. In our case study, we were interested in their social interactions at the cafeteria during their break times, so we adapted the methodology to our needs. We conducted 10 interviews with passers by in the area where the board was installed; 7 of them worked in the building, 1 worked for the same company in the same city but in a different location, 1 worked for the same company in another country, and 1 was a client visiting the building for the first time. The interviewees were between 21 and 54 years old, and all of them had smartphones.

To make sense of the data collected during the interviews, we used an Affinity Map, also known as the KJ Method [6,17], to infer interrelationships in the subjects' discourse by looking for patterns and common themes, opinions, and points of view. Two major groups of users emerged from this analysis: *insiders*, composed of individuals who work in the building where the tool was installed; and *outsiders*, whose opinions were neutral and therefore were not considered in this work.

The insiders were further divided in four categories: group **A**, with individuals who actually used the board, but only to follow news; group **B**, with users who did not use the board but had suggestions for improvements; group **C**, with users who did not use the board but liked the topic; and group **D**, with people who did not use the board and were unsatisfied with the topic. We employ this classification in order to organize opinions and suggestions from users below.

The main reason why users in groups **B**, **C** and **D** did not use the tool was the *topic*. Those in **D** explicitly mentioned this fact and said that, although the Board was visually appealing, carpooling was not interesting for them. Individuals in category **C** thought that carpooling is interesting but did not see themselves as potential users. Users in group **B** liked the tool, but were demotivated by the topic.

Interviewee #1, from group **B**, mentioned that the focus on carpooling might have decreased the interest people had in the technology and suggested that *it could be used to substitute a physical classified board* that was placed nearby and was typically used by employees to sell things. Interviewee #10, also from group **B**, conjectured that more people could have used the tool if *users were given the possibility to create topics*, i.e., to create their own instances of the board. Other concerns transmitted by users in group **B** evolve around three elements: *location, technology*, and *communication*.

Complains about *technology* clearly emerged from the fact that all the respondents had smartphones and would rather use Internet messages instead of SMS. This fact was reinforced by the quantitative analysis presented in Section 4.2 and remarks the main difference between the original target audience — individuals using entry-level cellphones — and the corporate environment.

Regarding *location*, for many respondents, the place where the panel was positioned was not ideal. Interviewee #7 said that it should be located not only in the cafeteria, but also in other areas where the flow of people is more intense. Other individuals suggested certain specific places that, in their opinion, would have fostered more participation.

Another issue was *communication*, in the sense that some users thought that the tool was focused solely on carpooling. That is, they were not aware of the existence of the other columns offered by the Board. Moreover, after a couple of months, the column that was used for news was substituted for another that were aimed at classified advertisements, but few people actually used it. Our quantitative and qualitative results suggest that more messages could have been posted if this change had been broadcasted in the building, so communication clearly plays an important role for technology adoption.

Group **A** shows that the Board had a large passive audience, composed of individuals who do not post messages but read what is being posted. Interviewee #4 was an interesting example of this group, since the person was able to discover that a former colleague who worked on the same department was actually living nearby her home and managed to get a ride just by checking the content posted in the board, that is, without sending a text message to the platform.

Finally, since we did not have access to active users, we analyzed the posts submitted to the platform in order to identify the topics that spontaneously emerged from interaction with the tool. Therefore, we considered only the messages that were posted in the Open Forum column. We employed context analysis [5] to make this classification and identified three main categories of messages according to their targets: a particular person or group of people; everybody who was reading the Board; and, finally, those who were actually submitted to the wrong column.

The existence of posts that were clearly placed in the wrong columns shows that the use of identification character is not intuitive and that an automatic message classifier should have been used instead. In particular, we believe that Latent Semantic Analysis [12] and Topic Modeling [9] probably would have produced satisfactory results.

Within the messages directed to the public, we identified four subtopics:

1. Greeting messages, such as "have a nice day" or "have a nice week";
2. "Check-in" messages, used by people to announce their break time and to say who was with them;
3. Contextual messages, talking about the weather or traffic conditions;
4. Messages about the Board.

Finally, the words appearing more frequently were "coffee" and "selling". The earlier shows that the Board location influenced message content, and the latter highlights the usability issues of the identification character.

4.2 Quantitative Approach

The feedback obtained from the qualitative studies indicated several issues in our deployment, specially with the choice of communication technology and theme. Nonetheless, we also observed that a range of other topics actually flourished in the space, leading us to believe that the Shared Message Board technology might be more valuable for purposes other than carpooling. To better understand this question, we conducted a survey focused on unveiling how professional communication takes place for other use cases. Through electronic forms, we solicited anonymous feedback from several subjects subscribed to internal and external mailing lists concerning their communication habits on work.

We collected data from 72 participants (25 female). Among them, 80% ranged between 18-35 years old, 15% between 36-55 and the remaining 5% above 56 years old; also 42% had between 0-5 years of work experience, 25% had 5-10, and 32% had over 10 years.

The questionnaire contained two main parts. The first consisted of reporting the usage frequency of a list of professional communication and peer exchange means – Facebook, LinkedIn, Twitter, e-mail, phone calls, instant messaging, SMS, face-to-face, enterprise notice/advertisement shared boards and intranet – on a scale of 1 (never use) to 5 (always use). The second part consisted of informing which of these means are employed in the following situations: *sharing hobbies, sharing an external event, looking for a new apartment, selling personal items to colleagues,* and also, *looking for a ride.*

In the first part of the survey, we tried to identify which communication tools are more generally used in the enterprise. The results show that there is a clear preference for *emails, phone calls, instant messaging,* and *face-to-face meetings.* Conversely, the usage rates of platforms such as Facebook, LinkedIn, and Twitter for the purpose were very low, suggesting that *informal means of communication are typically not employed in the enterprise.* This is an expected result, since these tools typically do not provide the level of privacy required by many companies.

In the second part, we assessed preferred communication channels in the enterprise for a number of purposes:

Sharing Interest about Hobbies: Facebook was a clear winner in this topic (preferred by 23%), followed by personal meetings (19%), and instant messaging (15%). Although apparently contradictory, given the answers to the first part of the survey, these results suggest that there is still a strong correlation between Facebook and instant messaging tools to personal activities.

Notifying Colleagues about External Events of Professional Interest: Email (27%) and Facebook (20%) where the tools of choice for this type of message. Companies employ mailing lists in order to facilitate the broadcast of this kind of information, so the prevalence of email is not surprising. Facebook "walls" are also suitable for notifications, since can be simultaneously visualized by several other users.

Looking for a New Apartment: In this case we had again major preference for Facebook (21%), personal meetings (16%), and instant messaging (16%). These results reinforce the association between Facebook and instant messaging with messages that have a stronger personal touch.

Looking for a Ride: Most users preferred personal meetings (19%) and instant messaging (17%). Twitter (13%), Facebook (12%), and Enterprise shared boards (11%) had smaller adoptions, while SMS (5%) was considerably lower. Carpooling clearly has a stronger personal aspect than the other elements, since it implies in personal meetings with a relatively long duration. Therefore, it is natural to expect that participants would be willing to know each other to a certain extent, and the results suggest that personal meetings and instant messaging are the best options according to most people. The fact that people were sharing the same work environment was not enough to overcome this barrier, and is most likely why the tool was not effective.

Selling Personal Items to Colleagues: For this type of activity, usage was nearly tied between Facebook (19%) and Enterprise shared boards (18%), followed by personal meetings (14%). Classifieds are more "asynchronous" and "impersonal", and also enable passive observation from people that are not necessarily acquainted with the users posting the content.

5   Discussion and Lessons Learned

The experiment, the interviews, and the survey allowed us to identify several important aspects associated to the use of shared message boards in the enterprise. Below, we discuss the results and extract some lessons we learned with this work.

Usage data extracted directly from the platform show that *community engagement is driven by need*. Shortly after the installation of the board, a storm occurred in the city where the company is placed. Since this phenomenon was correctly predicted by weather forecast services, people were aware of it beforehand. A couple of weeks later, we observed that this day registered the largest number of messages submitted to the platform. This fact suggests that certain events might nurture technology adoption once they are seen as the standard solutions to address them.

Regarding in-group communication for the enterprise, the results of our study show that *SMS-based communication is not adequate for corporate environments*. Since virtually every company is equipped with WiFi, *there is a clear preference for web-based applications*. Moreover, most people currently have smartphones, there is virtually no incentive for typically charged SMS services in the enterprise.

Additionally, we conclude that *shared message boards are not effective to support carpooling in Brazil*, since we observed that users still want to better know the people they are riding with. We initially believed that the proximity of being in the same company would overcome this barrier, but the results strongly suggest that this is not the case. It is important to remark that this might reflect a local cultural aspect, since there are relatively popular websites in other countries, such as Germany, providing this kind of service[1].

Finally, suggestions given during the interviews and the results of the survey indicate that *there are situations in which shared message boards might be an adequate communication tool for the enterprise*. In particular, we believe that shared message boards might reach higher adoption levels if used to broadcast non-personal information about topics that are not directly related with professional activities, such as classified advertisements.

6 Conclusions and Future Work

In this work, we presented and discussed the results of an experimented conducted in a large company in Brazil involving the use of a shared message board technology to support carpooling between its employees. Interviews and surveys helped us to identify the challenges and opportunities for this kind of tool in the enterprise.

The identification of use cases where shared message boards can be largely adopted in the enterprise and in other restricted communities is essential for the creation of personalized recommender systems, since they are able to generate a kind of human-generated data that is not being produced by the most popular communication tools, such as Facebook and Twitter. In particular, classified advertisement in the enterprise seems to be a promising application, so we believe that it would be interesting to conduct experiments with shared message boards applied to this usage.

Our ultimate goal is to apply analytics techniques (see [1,7]) to in-group and peer-based messages in order to identify the sentiments and learn the needs and requirements of restricted communities communities. Social Network Data Analytics tools [2] could be used to extract social intelligence from these interactions. In particular, we would like

---

[1] For example, *Mitfahrgelegenheit* (www.mitfahrgelegenheit.de) and *Mitfahrzentrale* (www.mitfahrzentrale.de).

to identify the main factors that influence technology adoption for in-group communication and the correlation between local context factors and communication behavior.

Acknowledgments. This work has been supported and partially funded by FINEP / MCTI, under subcontract no. 03.11.0371.00. Fernando Koch was working with IBM Research – Brazil during the time of this research.

References

1. Agarwal, A., Xie, B., Vovsha, I., Rambow, O., Passonneau, R.: Sentiment Analysis of Twitter data. In: Proceedings of the Workshop on Languages in Social Media, LSM 2011, pp. 30–38. Association for Computational Linguistics, Stroudsburg (2011)
2. Aggarwal, C.: Social Network Data Analytics, 1st edn. Springer Publishing Company, Incorporated (2011)
3. Archambault, A., Grudin, J.: A longitudinal study of Facebook, Linkedin, & Twitter use. In: Proceedings of the SIGCHI Conference on Human Factors in Computing Systems, CHI 2012, pp. 2741–2750. ACM, New York (2012)
4. Battestini, A., Setlur, V., Sohn, T.: A large scale study of text-messaging use. In: Proceedings of the 12th International Conference on Human Computer Interaction with Mobile Devices and Services, MobileHCI 2010, pp. 229–238. ACM, New York (2010)
5. Bauer, M., Gaskell, G.: Qualitative researching with text, image and sound. SAGE Publications (2010)
6. Bentley, F., Barret, E.: Building Mobile Experiences. MIT Press, Cambridge (2012)
7. Bermingham, A., Smeaton, A.F.: Classifying sentiment in microblogs: Is brevity an advantage? In: Proceedings of the 19th ACM International Conference on Information and Knowledge Management, CIKM 2010, pp. 1833–1836. ACM, New York (2010)
8. Beyer, H., Holtzblatt, K.: Contextual Design: Defining Customer-Centered Systems. Morgan Kaufmann (1988)
9. Blei, D.M.: Introduction to probabilistic topic models. Communications of the ACM (2011)
10. Brignall, H., Rogers, Y.: Enticing people to interact with large public displays in public spaces. In: Proceedings of INTERACT 2003, pp. 17–24 (2003)
11. Church, K., de Oliveira, R.: What's up with WhatsApp?: Comparing mobile instant messaging behaviors with traditional sms. In: Proceedings of the 15th International Conference on Human-computer Interaction with Mobile Devices and Services, MobileHCI 2013, pp. 352–361. ACM, New York (2013)
12. Deerwester, S., Dumais, S.T., Furnas, G.W., Landauer, T.K., Harshman, R.: Indexing by latent semantic analysis 41, 391–407
13. Greenberg, S., Rounding, M.: The notification collage: Posting information to public and personal displays. In: Proceedings of the SIGCHI Conference on Human Factors in Computing Systems, pp. 514–521. ACM (2001)
14. Johri, A.: Look ma, no email!: Blogs and IRC as primary and preferred communication tools in a distributed firm. In: Proceedings of the ACM 2011 Conference on Computer Supported Cooperative Work, CSCW 2011, pp. 305–308. ACM, New York (2011)
15. Le Dantec, C.: Participation and publics: Supporting community engagement. In: Proceedings of the 2012 ACM Annual Conference on Human Factors in Computing Systems, CHI 2012, pp. 1351–1360 (2012)
16. Lucero, A., Holopainen, J., Jokela, T.: MobiComics: Collaborative use of mobile phones and large displays for public expression. ACM Press (2012)

17. Martin, B., Hannington, B.: Universal Methods of Design: 100 Ways to Research Complex Problems, Develop Innovative Ideas, and Design Effective Solutions. Rockport Publishers (2012)
18. Molinaro, M., Borger, S., Cardonha, C., Gallo, D., Herrmann, R., Ferreira, A., Koch, F., Avegliano, P., Shigeno, K.: Smarter board: A community-oriented communication tool. In: Proc. of the 10th International Cross-Disciplinary Conference on Web Accessibility, W4A 2013 (2013)
19. Turner, T., Qvarfordt, P., Biehl, J.T., Golovchinsky, G., Back, M.: Exploring the workplace communication ecology. In: Proceedings of the SIGCHI Conference on Human Factors in Computing Systems, CHI 2010, pp. 841–850. ACM, New York (2010)
20. Vyas, D., Van De Watering, M.R., Eliëns, A., van der Veer, G.C.: Being social@ work: Designing for playfully mediated social awareness in work environments. In: Venkatesh, A., Gonsalves, T., Monk, A., Buckner, K. (eds.) Home Informatics and Telematics: ICT for the Next Billion. IFIP, vol. 241, pp. 113–131. Springer, Boston (2007)
21. Xu, A., Biehl, J., Rieffel, E., Turner, T., van Melle, W.: Learning how to feel again: Towards affective workplace presence and communication technologies. In: Proceedings of the SIGCHI Conference on Human Factors in Computing Systems, CHI 2012, pp. 839–848. ACM, New York (2012)

An Improved Learning Automata Approach for the Route Choice Problem

Gabriel de O. Ramos and Ricardo Grunitzki

Instituto de Informática
Universidade Federal do Rio Grande do Sul
Porto Alegre, RS, Brazil
{goramos,rgrunitzki}@inf.ufrgs.br

Abstract. Urban mobility is a major challenge in modern societies. Increasing the infrastructure's physical capacity has proven to be unsustainable from a socio-economical perspective. Intelligent transportation systems (ITS) emerge in this context, aiming to make a more efficient use of existing road networks by means of new technologies. In this paper[1] we address the route choice problem, in which drivers need to decide which route to take to reach their destinations. In this respect, we model the problem as a multiagent system where each driver is represented by a learning automaton, and learns to choose routes based on past experiences. In order to improve the learning process, we also propose a mechanism that updates the drivers' set of routes, allowing faster routes to be learned. We show that our approach provides reasonably good solutions, and is able to mitigate congestion levels in main roads.

1 Introduction

The increasing demand for efficient urban mobility is a major challenge in modern societies. Traditional approaches, like increasing the physical capacity, are unsustainable from many perspectives (e.g., economic, environmental). In this context, the concept of intelligent transportation systems (ITS) emerges as a means to make a more efficient use of existing road networks, trying to mitigate the need for increasing their physical capacity. The ITS are strongly related with the concept of smart mobility, which aims at promoting the use of technology to gather and integrate information in order to improve the efficiency of the transportation system [1]. Smart mobility has been advocated as one of the cornerstones in research related to smart cities.

One of the fronts towards ITS is concerned with correctly distributing the flow of vehicles into the network to avoid congestions. This kind of problem has been extensively studied by the traffic engineering community [2, 3], and is known as the traffic assignment problem (TAP). The TAP deals with distributing the flow of vehicles in a network regarding its capacity (a.k.a. supply) and the drivers' origins and destinations (OD-pairs, a.k.a. demand).

---

[1] A previous version of this work has appeared in the Fifth International Workshop on Collaborative Agents – Research & Development (CARE 2014).

F. Koch et al. (Eds.): CARE/AVSA 2014, CCIS 498, pp. 56–67, 2015.
© Springer-Verlag Berlin Heidelberg 2015

While traffic assignment is a reasonable approach for traffic engineering, it is not realistic from the drivers' viewpoint. The point here is that, conceptually, traffic assignment is performed by a central authority, which must have complete knowledge about the system as a whole. Although having a central authority is realistic for traffic supervision and infrastructure changes (long term planning), it might be unrealistic for assigning the day-to-day route of each driver (short term planning). The latter case can be referred to as route choice, in which a driver must choose among a set of possible routes from its origin to its destination. Studying the drivers' route choice behaviour is an important consideration to make a more efficient use of road networks [2]. Along these lines, many decentralized approaches have been proposed to the route choice problem, among which multiagent systems have been played a key role [4–6].

In this work, we approach the route choice problem from a multiagent learning perspective. We make use of the learning automata (LA) [7] theory, where a driver-agent (automaton) learns to choose its route based on past experiences. Each agent has a set with the K shortest routes among its origin and destination. The agents learn to choose among these routes using a learning scheme called linear reward-inaction, where routes are chosen with probability inversely proportional to their travel time (i.e., faster routes are more likely to be chosen).

We also propose a simple method to update the drivers' route sets, enabling agents to find alternative routes so as to improve their performance. Based on experiments, we show that our approach is able to find reasonably good solutions, contributing to make a more efficient use of the road network. Furthermore, the impact of our approach in an abstract road network is analysed, concluding that the congestion levels of main roads may be decreased.

Through this work, we aim at contributing towards the adoption of intelligent mechanisms to improve the drivers' decision making, which is aligned with the concept of smart mobility. From a practical perspective, our approach might be seen as an intelligent mobile service, which can be used by human drivers on their daily route choice process.

This paper is organised as follows. In Sect. 2 we present the related work. The problem is formulated in Sect. 3. Our approach is described in Sect. 4. The experiments and results are discussed and analysed in Sect. 5. Final remarks and future directions are presented in Sect. 6.

2 Related Work

Reinforcement learning is used to enable driver-agents to learn their routes in the work of Tavares and Bazzan [4]. To this end, a classical algorithm called Q-learning is used, which represents the environment as a Markov decision process and maps states into actions. In their approach, states are modelled as intersections, and actions as the links that leave the intersections. Through experiments, their approach has shown to be effective. However, as the route learning process is done through trial-and-error, the time required for the route to be learnt may be impractical in real situations. In our approach, we provide a number of alternative routes, among which the agent must learn the better one for him. In this sense, the drivers are able to learn much quicker.

An investigation of how traffic forecasts impact on drivers' decision making is made by Klügl and Bazzan [5], considering a two-route scenario. In their approach, drivers' route choice is based on a simple heuristic, which consists in selecting a route with probability proportional to its reward. A traffic control system is also proposed, which perceives drivers' decisions and returns a traffic forecast. Based on the forecast, drivers can change their routes before actually driving. The rationale behind the forecasts is to allow drivers to implicitly learn the usual decisions of other drivers. However, the scenario investigated is a quite simple, with just two possible routes. Furthermore, a centralized forecast provider is required.

Bazzan et al. [6] modelled route choice on the basis of the coordination game, where driver-agents deal with the problem of choosing between two routes. In their approach, agents are also able to form groups, and share information about their performance with their peers. In this sense, agents can choose the best route based on their peers' performance. However, such strategy may lead to congestions, since many drivers might choose the same route. Also, an investigation with more routes was left aside.

The route choice problem is addressed with a genetic algorithm by Cagara et al. [8]. In their approach, each driver has k possible routes to choose, which are encoded in a binary way. The individuals' chromosomes represent the routes assigned to each driver. Their approach, however, does not consider the real time experimented on each route, but the travel time under no congestion, which represents a naïve approach. Furthermore, the routes cannot be adapted to improve the drivers' efficiency. In our approach, both issues are appropriately addressed.

Pel and Nicholson [9] proposed a percentile-based route choice model, which assumes that drivers make decisions with respect to the route travel time distributions collected from past experience. In their approach, the focus is on identifying the amount of time that each driver must allocate to its trip in order to reach its destination on time. Considering the inherent variability of the routes travel times according the other drivers' decisions, it was identified that some agents are more sensitive to this variability than others. However, their approach is centralized.

From the traffic engineering perspective, the simplest assignment method is called all-or-nothing [2]. This method assigns the minimum cost (w.r.t. distance) routes to the drivers, assuming no congestion. Such assumptions are reasonable in sparse networks, in which just a few alternative routes are available. Although the all-or-nothing method may not be suitable in realistic scenarios, it has been used as a basis for more sophisticated traffic assignment approaches.

Along these lines, Ortúzar and Willumsen [2] have presented two iterative methods for finding approximate traffic assignment solutions based on all-or-nothing. The first method is the incremental assignment, where the drivers are incrementally assigned into routes, regarding the accumulated vehicles on them. This approach, however, does not allow the traffic to be rearranged so as to improve the final assignment. In this sense, the successive averages method was proposed, which uses an initial assignment based on free flow travel times. Through successive iterations, previous assignments form the basis to update the roads costs, and improve new assignments. However, both approaches are centralized.

The TAP and the road pricing problem (RPP) are jointly addressed by Buriol et al. [3]. Usually, the self-interested behaviour of drivers tends to lead to non-optimal solutions. In this sense, putting tolls in some roads can induce drivers to act in the behalf of a system optimal solution. Thus, RPP was introduced as a mean to achieve such behaviour. In their work, Buriol et al. used a random-key genetic algorithm to find solutions that bridge the gap between the drivers' and the system's optimal solutions. However, their approach depends on a high number of tolls to achieve good results, what may be impractical in economic terms. Furthermore, charging tolls is not a popular alternative from the drivers' viewpoint, although in some situations it may be essential.

As can be seen, many approaches do not consider the impact that agents' decisions and changes in the network have in the final results. Furthermore, many approaches do not provide methods that could be potentially used by drivers without requiring, e.g., a central authority assigning traffic. Our approach, on the other hand, uses an autonomous learning method that is able to consider the stochastic nature of the environment, which is more realistic from the drivers' perspective. Furthermore, our approach could be potentially implemented as an intelligent mobile service, which could be used by drivers in their daily route choice process.

3   Problem Formulation

A road network can be modelled as a directed graph $G = \{N, E\}$, where the set N of nodes represents the intersections, and the set E of edges represents the roads between intersections. Each edge $e \in E$ has a cost $c(e)$ associated with crossing it, like travel time or length. In this work, the cost function represents the travel time, and is defined according to Eq. (1) (as in [2]), where f_e and v_e are, respectively, the free flow travel time (minimum travel time when the edge is not congested), and the number of vehicles on the edge $e \in E$.

$$c(e) = f_e + 0.02 \times v_e \tag{1}$$

The flow of vehicles in a network is based on the amount of trips made between different origins and destinations (OD-pairs). A trip is made by means of a route $R \subseteq E$, which is a set of edges that connects an origin to a destination. The cost $C(R)$ of a given route R can obtained by summing up the costs associated with the edges that comprise it, as in Eq. (2).

$$C(R) = \sum_{e \in R} c(e) \tag{2}$$

In this work, the route choice problem is applied in a commuting scenario. A commuter driver repeatedly makes trips under approximately the same conditions (e.g., the daily routine of going to work). In this respect, each commuter is modelled as an agent (driver, henceforth), which repeatedly deals with the problem of choosing routes to make its trips. A driver $i \in D$ aims at choosing the route R that takes the least time to its destination. The utility of driver i when selecting a given route R is associated with the route's cost, as in Eq. (3), i.e., the higher the cost, the lower the utility.

$$u_i(R) = -C(R) \tag{3}$$

4 Method

In this work, the route choice problem is modelled from a LA perspective. A learning automaton (LA) is a reinforcement learning algorithm that attempts to improve agent actions' choice based on past actions, and on the received reinforcement signals. In this work, actions represent routes, and the reinforcement signal received for taking a route represents the utility associated with it. Along these lines, we can formalize a LA by a tuple $\langle \mathcal{R}_i, \pi_i, u_i, \mathcal{L} \rangle$, where:

- $\mathcal{R}_i = \{R_1, ..., R_K\}$ is the set of K routes (actions) available for agent i;
- $\pi_i : R \to [0, 1], R \in \mathcal{R}_i$, is a probability vector over agent i's actions; it is also called policy;
- $u_i : R \to [0, 1], R \in \mathcal{R}_i$, is the utility of agent i after taking route R, i.e., is the reward to be used as reinforcement signal;
- $\mathcal{L}$ is a learning scheme to update agents' π distributions.

A LA learns in episodes. In our approach, an episode is equivalent to a set of trips, one for each driver. Usually, a LA's episode is divided into two parts:

Route Choice, where agent i draws a random route $R \in \mathcal{R}_i$ according to its policy $\pi_i(R)$.
Policy Update, where the policy π_i is updated using the learning scheme $\mathcal{L}$ based on the received utility (reward) u_i, collected after finishing the episode.

Besides these two steps, in this approach we also employ a third one:

Route Set Update, where the set of routes of a given agent is recreated based on its experience.

The route choice step is based on the idea that drivers do not always take the route with highest expected utility. In this regard, routes with low utility are also chosen, though less likely than routes with higher utility. This is an important issue because the utility associated with the routes may change in time. In this sense, exploring other routes may bring benefits to the learning process.

The policy update step is performed after each episode based on the received utility, which is associated with the route taken. The update is made by means of a learning scheme $\mathcal{L}$. In this work, we use the well-known linear reward-inaction (L_{R-I}) scheme [7]. The L_{R-I} scheme updates the probability vector π_i according to Eq. (4), where $R^* \in \mathcal{R}_i$ is the route taken by agent i in the current episode, and $\alpha \in [0, 1]$ is the learning rate.

$$\pi_i(R) \leftarrow \pi_i(R) + \begin{cases} \alpha u_i(R)(1 - \pi_i(R)) & \text{if } R = R^* \\ -\alpha u_i(R)\pi_i(R) & \text{for the other routes} \end{cases} \tag{4}$$

In order to create the set of routes $\mathcal{R}_i$ of driver i, a classical algorithm called K Shortest Loopless Paths (KSP) [10] is used, which is able to find the K shortest routes between an OD-pair. Roughly speaking, the KSP algorithm starts with the shortest route, iteratively removing each edge from it and calculating a new route, until K shortest routes are found. The sets of routes are generated while creating the agents. At this time, the routes are generated considering free flow travel time[2] on edges, i.e., Eq. (1) with low values for v_e that still allow free flow travel time. Such an approach represents a suitable initial approximation for guiding the route choice policy. As the agents become experienced, however, the policy update step undertakes the task of incorporating the real edges' utility (reward) into the policy.

The policy update step improves on the route choice process by increasing the importance of routes that improve the agents' utilities. However, as the agents become experienced, alternative routes may prove appealing to them. Also, the utility of routes that were initially good may start to deteriorate with the increased flow of vehicles. In this sense, we also employ a route set update step, which is performed soon after the policy update step. To this end, each driver internally stores the mean costs experimented on each edge travelled, as shown in Eq. (5), where $\bar{c}_i(e)$ is the mean travel time experimented by agent i on edge e. Through this information, with small probability ω, each driver is able to rerun the KSP algorithm regarding their own estimations about edges travel times, and obtaining a new set of routes. Such an approach is used because, through experience obtained from previous episodes, drivers are able to find better routes. Furthermore, this mechanism promotes a higher diversity of routes (better distributing the flow of vehicles within the road network).

$$S_i = \{\langle e, \bar{c}_i(e) \rangle : e \in E\} \tag{5}$$

5   Experiments and Results

In order to evaluate the performance of our LA-based approach, we use the road network proposed by Ortúzar and Willumsen in the exercise 10.1 of their book [2] (OW10.1, henceforth). The OW10.1 network is composed by 13 nodes (named $A, B, ..., M$) and 24 bi-directed edges, as shown in Fig. 1, where the edges' numbers represent their free flow travel time (in minutes). The referred

---

[2] We assume that drivers are aware of the network topology (and also free flow travel times). This is a realistic assumption since this kind of information is already provided by navigation devices (such as GPS). On the other hand, drivers do not know in advance the traffic conditions on the network, what influence the real travel time on each edge.

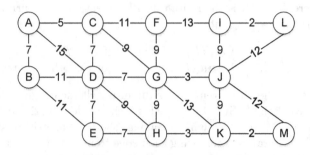

Fig. 1. OW10.1 road network (adapted from [2])

Table 1. Shortest routes (under no congestion) for each OD-pair, and respective costs under no congestion and when all drivers take the same route

OD-pair	Shortest route under no congestion	Route cost (min)	
		Under no congestion	With all-or-nothing assignment
AL	A - C - G - J - I - L	28	114
AM	A - C - D - H - K - M	26	78
BL	B - D - G - J - I - L	32	98
BM	B - E - H - K - M	23	55
Overall		27.06	88.82

network has four OD-pairs: AL, AM, BL, and BM, with demand of 600, 400, 300, and 400 vehicles, respectively. Experiments were conducted through macroscopic modelling and simulations. The drivers' performance is measured by means of the time spent on the trips to their destinations. The system's performance (overall travel time, hereafter) is represented by the average travel time of all drivers.

The OW10.1 network was chosen because it is small and has many problems related to routes overlapping. Table 1 presents, for each OD-pair, the shortest routes under no congestion, the cost under no congestion, and the cost due to the all-or-nothing assignment (which will be considered as a baseline in our experiments). As can be seen, if the route AL (second column of Table 1) were used by all the 600 drivers of AL pair, then its cost would increase from 28 to 115 minutes. Another important observation is that the BM route is much faster than others. This happens because the other pairs' routes are overlapping at least in some point. For example, in the second hop, node G receives flow from both pairs AL and BL pairs. At that specific point, 900 vehicles are trying to use the same edge GJ. In this respect, the OW10.1 network seems an interesting validation scenario.

In all experiments, the number of episodes was empirically set to 150. Each experiment was replicated 30 times, from which the average values and respective standard deviations were extracted. The values set to parameters K, ω, and α are discussed in Sect. 5.1. A comparison of our approach against others is presented in Sect. 5.2. Aspects concerning the learning convergence are discussed in Sect. 5.3. Finally, a brief study about the impact of our approach in the OW10.1 network is presented in Sect. 5.4.

5.1 Parameters

In this first set of experiments, we analyse the impact of the parameters K, α and ω in the systems' performance. First of all, we emphasize that results and conclusions presented here are based exclusively on the OW10.1 network, and do not necessarily hold in other networks without a further investigation.

We begin by trying different values for K and α, and deactivating our route set update step ($\omega = 0$). After experimenting different values for K, its impact on the result has shown inexpressive, although lower values have presented slightly better results. In this sense, the value $K = 4$ as been chosen, as it represents a good balance between the number of routes and the network topology.

Concerning parameter α, we concluded that its value does not have too much impact in the final result. On this basis, the impact of the routes set update step is firstly analysed. Recall that the routes set update step is responsible for enhancing the diversity of routes, and it is managed through parameter ω. With more routes being used, a more efficient usage of the network is expected. Figure 2a presents the impact of different values of ω in the results, with $K = 4$ and $\alpha = 0.1$. As shown, when routes sets are updated more frequently, the final result is improved. That is because higher values for ω increase the routes' diversity, i.e., more edges are explored. Consequently, the flow of vehicles is better distributed across the network.

The last parameter that has to be defined is the α. Different values of α were tested against different values of ω so as to find a suitable combination of values for these parameters. Figure 2b presents such results, with $K = 4$. As can be seen, increasing α slightly deteriorates the results. The rationale behind this

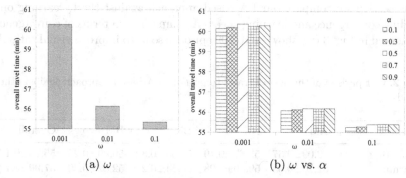

(a) ω (b) ω vs. α

Fig. 2. Overall travel time for different values of: ω, with $K = 4$ and $\alpha = 0.1$ (Fig. 2a); and ω vs. α, with $K = 4$ (Fig. 2b)

phenomenon is that lower learning rates lead the agents to be more conservative regarding their current policies. In other words, the agents tend to benefit more by exploiting their current knowledge. On the other hand, higher exploration rates tend to pose disturbances in the learning process, deteriorating the agents' utility.

Therefore, the best combination of parameters for this specific network is $K = 4$, $\alpha = 0.1$, and $\omega = 0.1$. These values are used in the next subsections' experiments.

5.2 Comparison against Other Methods

In this section we compare our LA-based approach with other methods from the literature. The focus here is on comparing the efficiency of the approaches on generating good solutions, from the perspective of the overall travel time measure. The methods used in the comparison are:

- Incremental and successive averages [2], two classical traffic engineering approaches for the traffic assignment problem.
- Q-learning for route choice. In this approach, no states are considered, and each agent has a set of K pre-computed routes, representing their available actions. The Q-learning parameters were empirically set as $\alpha = 0.8$, $\gamma = 0.9$, and $\epsilon = 1.0$ coupled with a decay rate of 0.925, which is multiplied by ϵ at the end of each episode.

The results are presented in Table 2. As can be seen, our approach outperforms the others. Compared to the traffic assignment methods described in [2], our approach has the advantage of being decentralized (i.e., it does not require a central authority), which is more realistic from the route choice perspective. Compared to Q-learning, the result of our approach is slightly better. Furthermore, the LA-based approach has a faster convergence (as shown in next section).

5.3 Convergence and Learning Speed

In this section we compare our LA-based approach against the Q-learning one regarding convergence and learning speed. A comparison in terms of convergence is presented in Fig. 3 (we show up to 100 episodes so as to improve visualisation).

Table 2. Comparison of the overall travel time of our LA-based approach against other methods

Method	AM	AL	BL	BM	Overall
LA-based	59.09±0.37	53.67±0.19	56.55±0.32	50.09±0.25	55.25±0.17
Q-learning	62.20±0.53	59.80±0.28	53.54±0.23	52.82±0.29	57.90±0.19
Incremental	69.92	58.36	73.24	57.36	64.83
Successive averages	70.92	64.82	68.90	62.21	67.08

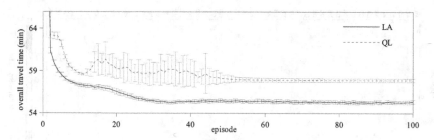

Fig. 3. Convergence time of our LA-based approach against Q-learning

The comparison takes place through the overall travel time along episodes. As shown, convergence was reached by our approach in less than 40 episodes. This occurs because the policy update scheme rapidly and efficiently learns the expected utility of each route. On the other hand, the Q-learning approach has to experiment an increased number of exploration episodes until a reasonable policy is found. Moreover, the Q-learning approach is very sensible to the exploration rate, which is not ruled by the agents' utility.

In terms of learning speed, our approach is also faster. The reason behind this behaviour relates to the fact that in our approach the set of K routes is not static, i.e., the set of routes varies from one agent to another. This feature is due to the route set update step, which can be improved based on the drivers' experience (according to parameter ω). Furthermore, the dynamics of the environment are indirectly embedded in the probability vector over the set of routes, which is used to guide the route choice. The Q-learning approach, in the other hand, has a static set of routes, thus less alternatives are explored.

5.4   Impact in the Network

In order to evaluate the impact of our approach in the OW10.1 network, we show how the edges occupancy varies along episodes. The occupancy rate of an edge is given by dividing the number of vehicles on it by its capacity[3]. When the occupancy rate of an edge nears 0, then there are few vehicles on it; on the other side, when an edge is under congestion, this rate nears 1. It should be noted that the occupancy rate may be larger than one. This is due to the fact that, in macroscopic simulations, the number of vehicles on a given edge is not constrained to its capacity (as observed in the literature [2]). However, albeit one may say that this measure is quite artificial, it is still a suitable approach to evaluate the congestions levels in the edges.

Figure 4 presents the edges' occupancy rate along episodes in a typical execution of our LA-based approach in the OW10.1 road network. The results

---

[3] The capacity of an edge is a function of its length. We estimate the length of an edge by assuming a maximum speed of 50km/h, and multiplying it by the edge's travel time under no congestion. In this sense, the capacity of a route may be approximated by dividing its estimated length by 5 (given that, in literature, 5m is a good approximation for the vehicles' lengths and the space between them).

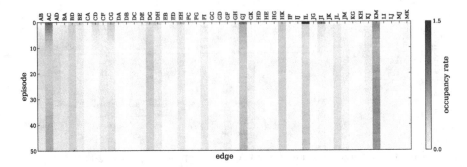

Fig. 4. Edges' occupancy rate along episodes

are presented by means of a heat-map. In the figure, horizontal axis represents the edges, and vertical axis represents the episodes. For each edge and episode, the plot shows the highest occupancy rate measured in the edge in that specific episode. In the plot, the darker the colour, the higher the occupancy rate. Results are shown for the 50 first episodes (where higher variations occur).

As shown in the plot, the occupancy rate of some edges is not improved along time, as is the case of edge KM. However, most of the edges have improved their occupancy rate. For instance, the initial occupancy rate of edge JI was of almost 0.9 (high congestion). However, after our approach was used, such a rate dropped to 0.06. This improvement confirms our initial hypothesis that, as drivers learn to choose their routes, the use of the road network becomes more efficient.

Another important observation regards the fact that some edges have worsen their occupancy rate (e.g., edge AD). That is a natural effect of distributing the drivers into the road network. In the initial scenario (all drivers taking the same routes), just a few edges absorb all the network flow, and all the unused edges have a zero occupancy rate. However, as the traffic is distributed across the network, part of the flow of vehicles is diverted from the most used edges into those that were not being used before. Therefore, it is clear that the aim here is not on reducing the occupancy rate of all edges, but distributing the flow in a way that the drivers' utility, and also the overall network utility, is maximized.

6   Conclusions

In this paper, we have presented a multiagent approach to address the route choice problem. The problem is approached from a LA perspective, where driver-agents learn to choose routes based on past experience. The set of routes is given in advance to the agents, and their learning scheme is based on the linear reward-inaction algorithm. A simple route set update is proposed, which promotes routes' diversity. Through experiments, we have shown that our approach provides reasonably good solutions, and is able to make a more efficient use of the road network. A key point of our approach related to traditional ones, is that ours does not require a central authority assigning traffic. Instead, we make use of learning techniques that allow the traffic elements (drivers, in this case) to improve their, and system's, efficiency. Furthermore, our approach might be potentially implemented as an intelligent mobile service to guide the drivers' daily route choice process.

For future work, we would like to investigate information exchange mechanisms, like inter-vehicular communication (IVC). Through IVC, agents can improve their knowledge about network conditions, and also can benefit from social interactions. Another interesting direction would be enhancing the route set update mechanism. An alternative in this direction would be replacing the probability selection (with ω) by a domain aware criterion (e.g., if the performance of a driver deteriorates below a given rate). Modelling the network performance in the agents' utility also represents a promising direction. Finally, other algorithms for learning (instead of L_{R-I}) and routes generation (instead of KSP) may be a good step towards improving our approach.

Acknowledgments. The authors are very grateful to Ana Bazzan and the anonymous reviewers for their valuable comments. Gabriel de O. Ramos and Ricardo Grunitzki are partially supported by SENAT/ITL.

References

1. Bazzan, A.L., Klügl, F.: Introduction to Intelligent Systems in Traffic and Transportation. Synthesis Lectures on Artificial Intelligence and Machine Learning, vol. 7. Morgan and Claypool(2013)
2. Ortúzar, J., Willumsen, L.G.: Modelling Transport, 3rd edn. John Wiley & Sons (2001)
3. Buriol, L.S., Hirsh, M.J., Pardalos, P.M., Querido, T., Resende, M.G., Ritt, M.: A biased random-key genetic algorithm for road congestion minimization. Optimization Letters 4, 619–633 (2010)
4. Tavares, A.R., Bazzan, A.L.C.: Independent learners in abstract traffic scenarios. Revista de Informática Teórica e Aplicada 19(2), 13–33 (2012)
5. Klügl, F., Bazzan, A.L.C.: Route decision behaviour in a commuting scenario. Journal of Artificial Societies and Social Simulation 7(1) (2004)
6. Bazzan, A.L.C., Fehler, M., Klügl, F.: Implicit coordination in a network of social drivers: The role of information in a commuting scenario. In: Tuyls, K., Jan't Hoen, P., Verbeeck, K., Sen, S. (eds.) LAMAS 2005. LNCS (LNAI), vol. 3898, pp. 115–128. Springer, Heidelberg (2006)
7. Narendra, K.S., Thathachar, M.A.L.: Learning Automata: An Introduction. Prentice-Hall, Upper Saddle River (1989)
8. Cagara, D., Bazzan, A.L.C., Scheuermann, B.: Getting you faster to work - A genetic algorithm approach to the traffic assignment problem. In: Proc. of the 16th Annual Conf. on Genetic and Evol. Comp. (Companion), New York (2014)
9. Pel, A.J., Nicholson, A.J.: Network effects of percentile-based route choice behaviour for stochastic travel times under exogenous capacity variations. In: Proc. of the 16th Intl. IEEE Annual Conf. on Int. Transp. Systems, pp. 1864–1869 (2013)
10. Yen, J.Y.: Finding the k shortest loopless paths in a network. Management Science 17(11), 712–716 (1971)

Urban Context Detection and Context-Aware Recommendation via Networks of *Humans as Sensors*

Sergio Alvarez-Napagao, Arturo Tejeda-Gómez, Luis Oliva-Felipe,
Dario Garcia-Gasulla, Victor Codina, Ignasi Gómez-Sebàstia,
and Javier Vázquez-Salceda

Universitat Politècnica de Catalunya, Barcelona, Spain
{salvarez,jatejeda,loliva,dariog,vcodina,igomez,jvazquez}@lsi.upc.edu

Abstract. The wide adoption of smart mobile devices makes the concept of *human as a sensor* possible, opening the door to new ways of solving recurrent problems that occur in everyday life by taking advantage of the information these devices can produce. In the case of this paper, we present part of the work done in the EU project SUPERHUB and introduce how geolocated positioning coming from such devices can be used to infer the current context of the city, *e.g.*, disruptive events, and how this information can be used to provide services to the end-users.

Keywords: social networks, smart mobile devices, human as a sensor, recommender systems.

1 Introduction

Mobility is one of the main challenges for urban planners in cities. Even with the constant technological progress, it is still difficult for policy makers and transport operators to 1) know the state of the city in (near) real-time, and 2) achieve proximity with the end-user of such city services, especially with regards to communicating with the citizen and receiving proper feedback.

There is a relatively recent technological advance that enables an opportunity to partially tackle these issues: ubiquous computational resources. For instance, thanks to smartphones, users that move in a city can potentially generate automatic data that may be hard to obtain otherwise: location, movement flow, average trip times, and so on. Moreover, transport network problems and incidents that affect mobility services are often documented by someone somewhere in the Internet at the same time or even before, than they appear in official sources or in the news media. This phenomenon has been referred to as *humans as sensors* [14]. Sensing through mobile humans potentially provides sensor coverage where events are taking place. An additional benefit is that human expertise can be used to operate such sensors to raise the quality of measurements, through *e.g.*, a more intelligent decision making, such as setting up a camera in an optimal way in poor lighting conditions; or providing exploitable additional metadata, as in collaborative tagging processes such as hashtagging.

F. Koch et al. (Eds.): CARE/AVSA 2014, CCIS 498, pp. 68–85, 2015.
© Springer-Verlag Berlin Heidelberg 2015

In this paper, we show a system that is able to mine such data in order to:

1. improve knowledge obtained from other data generation approaches, such as GPS pattern analysis,
2. detect unexpected situations in the city that may affect large groups of people at a certain location, *e.g.*, public demonstrations or celebrations, sudden traffic jams caused by accidents, and
3. enable services to users that exploit such generated knowledge, providing novel kinds of real-time information and recommendation.

The paper presents, due to space constraints, just a general overview of the problems we tackle, the preliminar results of the parts already implemented, and the future work. For deeper reports on the technical details, please refer to the related deliverables[1] and to [8].

This paper is structured as follows: in §2 we introduce SUPERHUB, an urban mobility-related EU project; §3 contains an explanation of the extent of the contextual detection, focusing on social network data; §4 explains how the contextual information generated can be used to provide services for the end-users; and finally §5 presents related work and wraps up the paper with conclusions.

2   The Case of SUPERHUB

SUPERHUB [2] is a project co-funded by the European Commission. Its main goal is to provide an open platform capable of considering in real time various mobility offers, in order to provide a set of mobility services able to address users' needs. At the same time the project intends to promote user participation and environmental friendly and energy-efficient behaviours.

To achieve these objectives SUPERHUB is developing, but not limited to (see Figure 1):

- a persuasive engine based on captology principles to facilitate the voluntary adoption of environmentally-friendly multi-mobility habits,
- novel methods and tools for real-time reasoning on large data streams coming from heterogeneous sources;
- new algorithms and protocols for inferring traffic conditions from mobile users, by coupling data from mobile phone networks with information coming from both GPS data and social network streams; and
- mechanisms for dynamic matchmaking of resources, and
- a journey planner with the goal of best fulfilling user mobility needs and preferences while minimizing negative environmental impact.

In SUPERHUB, users play an active, consumer and producer role (*prosumer*), acting, on the one hand, as providers of mobility offers, such as in car-pooling negotiations, and on the other hand, and more importantly for the purpose of this document, as consumers of mobility resources, such as taking the bus, using a public parking, or renting a bike).

---

[1] http://www.superhub-project.eu/downloads/viewcategory/
6-approved-deliverables.html

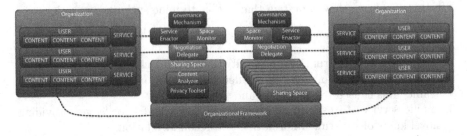

Fig. 1. *Persuasive mobility Services and Interfaces* view of the SUPERHUB architecture [4]. In boxes, the components this paper focuses on.

The project builds on the notion that citizens are not just mere users of mobility services, but represent an active component and a resource for policy-makers willing to improve sustainable mobility in smart cities. Existing journey planners only provide a few options to let users customize, to some extent, how the journey should look like. The reality, however, is more nuanced – different users might prefer different routes which, in addition, depend on the users context (*e.g.*, a shopping trip, travelling with small children or going back home) as well as on the environmental context: weather, traffic, crowdedness, events, *etc.* Specifying all of the circumstances affecting what the user perceives as the ideal plan, however, would be overwhelming.

Fig. 2. Screenshot of the SUPERHUB mobile app

The SUPERHUB planner employs the state of the art user modelling and recommender systems techniques – by observing the past users choices and the context in which these choices were made, SUPERHUB gradually learns the model that accurately reflects the multifaceted nature of each users preferences and constraints. During a journey plan search, the user model is used, in addition to the automatically acquired contextual information, to guide the search process in order to provide highly-tailored journey plan recommendations that best reflect the unique needs and situational context of each user. Technically, the personalization process relies on a mixture of contextual content-based filtering plus the use of semantics applied to contextual data, thus being able to assess different contexts, even if these have not been experienced by the user yet.

In addition, journey plans are further personalized by means of opportunistic recommendation. The SUPERHUB opportunistic recommender enhances journey plans by adding points of interest that might be interesting for the user during the journey. For example, if the user is going back home and she has to wait to take the train, the recommender may suggest having a coffee or doing some small shopping. In some circumstances, the recommender may even suggest alternative destinations (*e.g.*, a different cinema or supermarket) if the original destination is difficult to reach in current traffic conditions.

The Intelligent Mobility Recommender combines state-of-the-art recommendation algorithms and data representation allowing the creation of personalized trip recommendations which best reflecting the user's contextual situation, needs and preferences. The recommender uses the latest developments in hybrid recommendation, combining semantically-enhanced content-based approaches with social advanced collaborative filtering approaches based on user clustering and user similarity. This allows for additional personalization of journeys beyond the capabilities of the journey planner alone.

The Intelligent Mobility Recommender (IMR) also allows opportunistic recommendation: suggestions that go beyond the change of journey routing alone, *e.g.*,, postponing the trip or choosing an alternative equivalent destination if current conditions would make accommodating the request too costly. Most importantly, the IMR incorporates algorithms to proactively support this kind of recommendation, whenever conditions, automatically detected from the context, are favourable to fulfilling user's mobility goals.

This is reflected in the project Description of Work, as one of SUPERHUB top-level primary objectives is to provide user-tailored mobility services, able to combine in real-time all available mobility offers to present a number of route options to end-users, ranked according to users preferences and environmental impact.

At a technical level, this is reflected in a front-end component of the system that automatically builds, maintains and adapts users profile over time, which includes a detailed description of users preferences in terms of mobility options. The profile is used to customize and rank mobility offers, in such a way to promote solutions as close as possible to users expectations, in terms of their needs and goals, while fostering the adoption of environmentally-friendly offers.

SUPERHUB provides an open platform, through which users inquire for possible mobility options to reach a given destination at any given time. The back-end system replies providing a rich set of possible options and recommendations taking into account a number of mobility solutions. The possible options are ranked based on the preferences elaborated within the user's profile, which includes information such as the perceived importance of the environmental impact, the willingness to walk/cycle in rainy weather etc. After the choice is made by the user, the system tracks and guides the user throughout her/his journey and constantly offers, at run time, new options/suggestions to improve the service experience, for example assisting her/him in the search of the nearest parking lot or providing her/him additional and customised information services such as pollutions maps.

This component will be subsequently used to offer concrete travel recommendations and directions by dynamically matching travel requests with the available mix of transport options. This process will take into account the user profile, situational context and current traffic situation, transport resources available, and mobility policies. All of these elements are gathered and processed in the scope of SUPERHUB. Additionally, journey recommendations generated by the planner will be used by the persuasive engine that will try to push the user towards more sustainable mobility habits.

3   Real-Time Detection of Urban Context

In a real-world setting, the SUPERHUB journey planner has to be ready to receive high amounts of journey plan requests and deliver multimodal recommendations that best fit a wide range of criteria, including user preferences. However, the evaluation of such criteria is continuously dependent on factors that occur in the external world, what we call the context of the request. And the context, given the same external conditions, is always city-dependent.

For example, if a request for a journey plan is made in January while it is snowing, in the case of Helsinki it is considered a normal situation and public transport should not be affected by such weather conditions. However, if the user is in Barcelona it is considered an extraordinary case that has numerous, unpredictable consequences on the transport networks. Therefore, weather sensor data may be useful to detect a context, but is not sufficient by itself.

3.1   From Heterogeneous Sensor Data to Real-Time Knowledge

This process is being carried in SUPERHUB by the Semantic Interpreter, taking advantage of semantic interpretation techniques in order to infer knowledge from both situational and historical data. Such knowledge can be applied by other components for diverse purposes, such as generating more fine-grained user models, or being able to understand normality with respect to policy fulfillment and thus derive and predict unexpected situations.

However, receiving heterogeneous data in a common model does not mean that the situational data is specified at the same level of abstraction or granularity. For instance, a subset of the SUPERHUB adaptors belong to the field of web-based social networks, with content typically expressed in plain text. Some intermediate steps (based in NLP semantic extraction techniques) must be followed in order to extract a structured concept representation of the meaning of the raw data.

More generally, data has to be normalised, so that values used in the representation of the data belong to the same abstract data type ranges; and aggregated, so that data that comes from potentially unreliable sources can be contrasted and therefore reinforced or discarded. Expert knowledge in the form of input models, such as the model of the city, designed by mobility experts, is converted into rules that will be used to infer a first abstraction of knowledge.

The Semantic Interpreter works at two levels of memory: a short-term memory and a long-term memory. The first one is a time window ending at the current point of time, the size of which is determined by the time, location and semantic content of the most relevant recent situational data. The second one is a complete set of historical data, which has to be maintained in order to avoid potentially infinite memory space consumption. The combination of the use of rules and a two-stage memory brings about the possibility of using compact representations of semantic content, such as RDF triples in triple-stores, or in distributed document or key-valued stores. In SUPERHUB we use a mix of these technologies in order to optimise the use of the resources.

In summary, The Semantic Interpreter is a component that provides knowledge in the form of RDF triples inferred from sensor data that is of a higher level of abstraction than what is usually obtained with other techniques, acting as a central point for data homogenisation. Via the Semantic Interpreter, raw data is filtered, normalised and interpreted into high-level concepts. Such concepts can be merged and analysed to generate derivative concepts that are not explicit in the sensor data but implicit in the aggregation of large instances of it. The analysis relies in applying semantic inference via Pellet, fed by expert knowledge and constitutive information about the city in SWRL, applied to statistical aggregations.

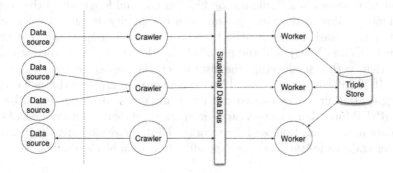

Fig. 3. Sketch of the internal components of the Semantic Interpreter

The SUPERHUB Semantic Interpreter has been implemented in Clojure [10] (a dialect of Lisp) and has been collecting and processing data on top of the JVM since July 2013. The raw data, in a normalised form (called *Situational Data*) is stored in MongoDB as JSON documents, while the RDF produced representing high-level knowledge, *e.g.*, disruptive events, are stored in a Neo4j graph database. Internally, the implementation is based on independent, autonomous agents that communicate with each other exclusively by asynchronous messages via *Clojure agents*. The agents have the capability of proactively assign themselves a particular role (see Figure 3):

- *Crawler* agents assign themselves a target API or web service and manage the reception of data from them, coordinating between them which endpoints from a common pool should be queried or listened to next, and

- *Worker* agents schedule periodical aggregation processes. Aggregation processes can be hot-plugged and removed from the Semantic Interpreter at runtime via plug-ins, and can include but are not limited to: crowdedness by area and time interval, crowdedness by Point of Interest and time interval, user trajectories by time interval, disruptive events detection, *etc.*

In a data-sensible application such as the Semantic Interpreter, reliability is a crucial feature. In our system agents are fail-safe in the sense that if a process fails, another agent is taken from a pool to automatically select one or more roles and fulfill them. Scalability is handled by the Semantic Interpreter by not allowing more agents than $n - 1$, where n is the number of cores of the host. The system handles tasks in an abstract way, while the execution part is held autonomously by agents that can plan individually and coordinate between themselves. Therefore, the system is decentralised and scheduled tasks are always picked up, and a result of that failures in the Semantic Interpreter have been very sporadic (two shortages in 7 months).

An instance of the Semantic Interpreter can be parametrised by setting up the following values in a configuration file: latitude and longitude of the central coordinate, radius of the metropolitan area of the city, counts-as rules (city-specific interpretation rules in RDF), social network API keys, the credentials to MongoDB and Neo4j, and the periodicity of the aggregation processes. This means that, with a small setup, the instance can be applied to any city.

The RDF information generated by the Semantic Interpreter through each of the aggregation processes carried out by agents is visually represented by the SUPERHUB Situational Data Visualiser. In Figure 4 there is an example of such information: raw data from social networks (dots), density by area (rectangles), and user trajectories (arrows) corresponding to a span of 15 minutes.

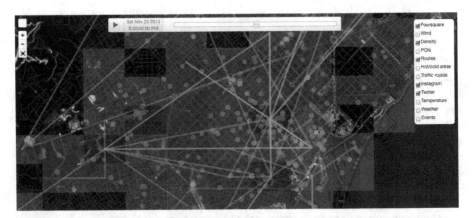

Fig. 4. Screenshot of the SUPERHUB Situational Data Visualiser, showing raw data, density by areas and user trajectories

3.2 Inferring City Context from Social Networks

In SUPERHUB, many types of sensors and services are used to get a picture of what is going on in the city: GPS real-time data, mobility flow patterns, official alerts, social network information propagation and weather forecasts among others. Each of these kinds of situational data come in their own format and dealing with a distinctive set of concepts, that is: speaking their own language. By simply combining incoming loads of such data, it is not possible to make pertinent complex decisions. We need something more than just a raw data-based picture of the city: we need to infer what the big picture is in order to interpret the current context and its implications. After that we will be able to detect relevant situations.

Basically, a normal situation in the city can be modelled under a spatio-temporal context which can be defined as any information that characterises a situation. It means that a day of a week, weather conditions, city zone (geolocation) and the type of road could be part of this context. For instance: traffic could be different on Monday at 7:00 am compared to Saturday at the same time; between two different weather conditions: rainy or sunny; or the type of road: highway or boulevard, etc. However, to monitor an entire city with several type of sensors for discovering disruptive events and incidents may not be affordable.

Alternatively, a *human as a sensor* approach brings a new opportunity to minimize the cost and reveal information that cannot be extracted directly from others sensors. If there is a traffic jam or accident that traffic jam cameras can detect but not explain the cause, why not get it from social networks? Social media applications are fast growing in recent years and now users reports real-life events all day long. Some of them allow users to include their geolocation which is relevant to pinpoint where the reported event occurred.

In SUPERHUB, many types of situational data are retrieved from different sensors: weather, traffic and social networks. From social networks data sources such as: Twitter (microblogging), Instagram (microblogging) or Foursquare (location-based) are combined in order to provide the normal situations in the city in terms of population density. Based on user's geolocated posts, we are able to identify: which are the main points of interests, how the people move along the city on their daily basis or before/after an event occurs (trajectories), and specific mobility user profiles (*e.g.*, tourists). Besides that, other data sources could be cross referenced with social networks data in order to filter noisy information, provide reliability, add explanations about events and validate the results of the detection system.

Disruptive events and incidents in the mobility city field are abnormal situations that have a significant impact on the city mobility, for instance: traffic jams or metro service delays. In order to maintain a reliable mobility city behaviour, it is necessary to detect and predict these kind of events.

In the case of Twitter, tweets are aggregated and analysed in time windows in order to find located trends [15]. In information diffusion, reliability of data obtained is a big concern, and our solution is to filter bots and spammers by analysing the topology of the individual social networks of the users [1], and by calculating their influence on other users [9]. The Foursquare API adds to the reliability score of the aggregated data by contrasting the detected trends against area-based collections of check-ins in the same time windows.

The mobility experts partners in SUPERHUB have an important role in the process of situation detection: once a trend has been detected, it is stored and presented to stakeholders so that they can tag whether it is really a situation and, if so, whether it is important to detect similar situations in the future. The information retrieved from experts is subsequently stored as feedback in a case-based knowledge base that improves the efficiency of trend detection.

Currently, the Semantic Interpreter is able to detect disruptive events based on abnormal social network activity. By grounding the model of events spatio-temporally we build a representation of each event which allows temporal and spatial reasoning. Our final event representation, further discussed in [8], allows us to know the relevance of the event (how much it deviates from expected behavior), the impact of the event (what is its effect on nearby areas and mobility services) and how the event forms and disperses (when did the event actually begin, when it reached full certainty, when did it began to fade away and for how long) among others. All those features together with the results of a collaborative tagging process (see §3.3) empowers interesting features, supported by promising results. As an example of those consider the most relevant events detected by the system (those with a higher deviation from the expected behavior). The top 40 events are shown in Table 1.

Another example of potential application of this methodology is that of *event crowd estimation*. Since Table 1 indicates that events detected with more certainty are those with more popular assistance, we considered the possibility of estimating the actual assitance to an event through the data collected by our system. We obtained the estimated assistance to the top 100 events detected from official sources when available, and estimated the rest from venue capacity. The result is a dispersion chart showing the relationship between the average activity captured by our system and the actual attendance of the event, along with a computed linear regression (see Figure 5). The Pearson correlation coefficient is approximately 0.82, which is a relevant result considering the dispersion of the data collected. This experiment suggests that we can automatically estimate the number of people at an event through its representation in our model.

3.3   User Input as a Basis for Interpretation

Disruptive event detection is not a simple process: it requires extensive storage and processing capacity. The identification of disruptive events does not depend solely on several data sources which have to be aggregated, analyzed and possibly tagged by experts and learned by a computational system, but also relies on the reliability of the source and a previous detection of what is normal.

When disruptive events happen – *e.g.*, accident, traffic jam, sports events, public demonstrations, flashmobs –, in most cases it will be captured by the SUPERHUB system thanks to the combination of heterogeneous data sources. However, in many cases there is no further available information that can explain

Table 1. Top 40 events by impact and their description. FCB stands for FC Barcelona (football, basketball) and RCDE stands for RCD Espanyol (football).

Rank	Event description	Rank	Event description
1	FCB vs Madrid	11	3 nearby concerts
2	FCB vs Elche	12	Airport
3	FCB vs Malaga	13	Michael Buble concert
4	FCB vs RCDE	14	Arctic Monkeys concert
5	FCB vs Milan	15	New Year @ Park Guell
6	FCB vs Granada	16	Airport
7	FCB vs Valencia	17	Bruno Mars concert
8	FCB vs Villareal	18	FCB vs Efes (Basketball)
9	FCB vs Celtic	19	FCB vs Real Sociedad
10	FCB vs Cartagena	20	Airport
21	Depeche Mode concert	31	Barcelona Fashion Week
22	New Year @ Park Guell	32	FOALS concert
23	Daughter concert	33	Christmas shopping
24	RCDE vs Madrid	34	Biffy Clyro concert
25	Airport	35	FCB vs Real Sociedad
26	Parc Guell visit	36	Mishima concert
27	FCB vs Getafe	37	Airport
28	New Year @ Sagrada Familia	38	RCDE vs Madrid
29	New Year @ Placa Espanya	39	FCB vs Levante
30	Camp Nou visit	40	Lori Meyers concert

exactly what happened than a geolocated position. Social networks and user inputs can be used as part of the disruptive event detection process.

In addition to provide context on past events, visualization (see Figure 4) can be the first step to identify by mobility observers when a disruptive event arises or any planned event becomes an unexpected one.

Where official or trusted sources are not sufficient to explain or depict an event, we can use social network messages to understand an event, if the source has a history of reliable reporting, where their previous reports matched past events, or were widely shared (retweeted).

We take advantage of stakeholders and users as experts that annotate and learn about detected events to identify and predict them. Users can inform and provide context about events in real-time, as well as provide tagging information of unclassified past events. In such cases, the identification of recurrent events allow the classification of what is normal and what is not. Currently, user feedback is retrieved by providing a collaborative tagging web application (see Figure 7). In this applications, users are presented random disrupted events (or they pick a specific one from the Situational Data Visualiser), and by using an autocomplete control they assign tags that are linked to RDF concepts. These concepts currently include DBPedia, WordNet RDF, and an *ad hoc* ontology of Points of Interest based on the Foursquare API.

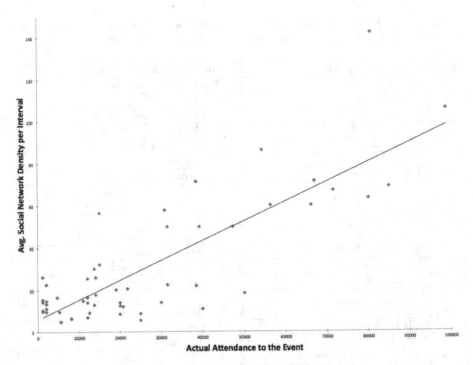

Fig. 5. Captured data vs. actual attendance for the Top 100 events detected

3.4 Taking Advantage of Mobile Devices to Refine Local Interpretation

Currently, the SUPERHUB Android mobile app includes a lightweight interface that communicates with the journey planner API. One of the features that this app provides is the possibility of reporting a disruptive event, by choosing options specified in a taxonomy. The mobile app also sends, if the user explicitly authorises so, GPS traces with the positioning of the user accross time. As future work, and taking advantage of the fact that the Semantic Interpreter is easily configurable and automatically scalable, we plan to embed a small and lightweight version of the Semantic Interpreter instance, working transparently as a low-priority background process. This instance can be used to obtain more detailed data coming from the social networks by setting up a smaller radius as a parameter[2], and to perform basic aggregation processes.

Figure 8 shows an schema of this proposal: the instance responsible for the whole city is in charge of maintaining in real-time a list of all mobile app-embedded Semantic Interpreter and exposing an API for its Triple Store. Mobile-embedded

---

[2] This is due to the fact that the public APIs of the social networks have request limitations per each API key. Users of the mobile app have the option to provide connection to social networks, and this connection can be used to obtain more fine-grained data, virtually expanding the city-wide Semantic Interpreter capabilities.

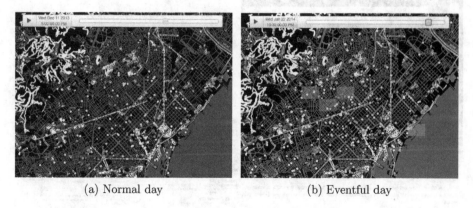

(a) Normal day   (b) Eventful day

Fig. 6. Difference between a normal day and a day with several events happening at the same time. Coloured (or grey) rectangles indicate the grid areas where a disruptive event was happening at that exact moment.

instances are connected between themselves, understanding the position of the nearest ones and thus dynamically deciding whether to expand or shrink their radius of data gathering.

4   Context-Aware User-Centric Services

The use of personalization in the field of journey planning is mainly focused on tourism [13]. Although there are other domains where routes are also recommended, e.g., for sporting/leisure purposes [5,11]. For instance, [5] produces journey hiking walkways according to a set of milestones or personalize journey plans by choosing from pre-defined routes which better fit users preferences. Afterwards, the selected routes are enhanced by means of adding Points Of Interest (POI) -relevant geographical features that may be relevant to the user.

In general, these approaches can be considered as aimed at providing routes to users on closed domains, that is: 1) the set of potential journey plans is already defined, and 2) the journey plans are built based on a recommended set of POIs (e.g., touristic routes). Other approaches try to overcome this closed domain constraint. While some solutions successfully generate this kind of routes, they do not incorporate users preferences or just a small set of generic preferences are taken into account (e.g., departure time or cost) [12].

SUPERHUB aims to generate journey plans from a more open perspective. Users select a destination and plans are designed accordingly, using different modes of transport, including car-pooling, and considering users preferences and contextual information (e.g., weather and current users situation). Consequently, the routes are not enclosed to contain certain POIs and the space search is broader and more complex.

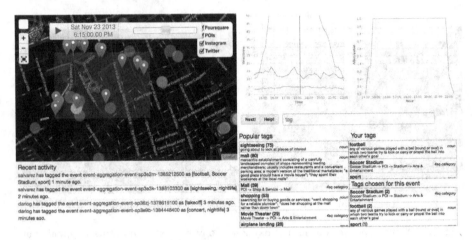

Fig. 7. Screenshot of the app for collaborative tagging of disruptive events

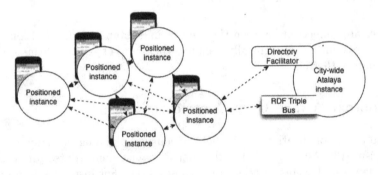

Fig. 8. Schema of a distributed system of Semantic Interpreters

The objective of our recommender is two-fold: 1) recommending journey plans, and 2) providing opportunistic recommendations in real-time. A good example of both functionalities can be found in [5]. Our recommender differs from that approach in that routes are not taken from a pre-defined set, but are dynamically generated according to contextual situation in the city. Thus, [5] adds a set of POIs to enhance the routes which is similar to our approach for opportunistic recommendation, although it does not take into consideration contextual information.

As discussed previously in §2, the SUPERHUB recommender makes use of contextual data to perform context-aware recommendations. When context matters, as is the case of the mobility domain – *e.g.*, when it is raining, people generally prefer to avoid walking or riding a bike –, it is sensible to use a user model that has been learnt with feedback acquired in the same context as the target user, as only that feedback is relevant for the prediction.

Given the different nature of both functionalities - predicting user satisfaction towards a suggested journey plan and suggesting appealing POIs along a route - our recommender system implements two different recommender algorithms to

Fig. 9. Screenshot of the opportunistic recommender of the SUPERHUB journey planner

provide them. In one hand, predicting user score towards journey plans; ideally, there is a large amount of possible Journey Plans or Legs. This implies that any feedback retrieved from users may be too sparse, which makes difficult to find similar users to proceed with a collaborative-filtering approach (*e.g.*, only users that perform the same routes would be found as similar users). Our solution adopts a content-based approach, which is consistent with current state of the art on mobility recommenders. By means of extracting features that define a Journey Plan or Leg, it is possible to learn the preference towards each feature from users feedback given to previous journey plans. For instance, a user may provide positive feedback towards journey plans that require little walking and mainly use the bus at night, and negative feedback to journey plans that require walking or riding a bike also when it is dark. Therefore, we can predict better score to journey plans that include taking the bus when night rather than walking. It is worth noticing that user may have explicited the preference towards riding a bike or a bus, but the user model has learnt the preference about the same modes of transport under different contexts. Thus, the training process incorporates users preferences as a starting point and process feedback from previous journey plans done to refine those preferences. In the other hand, suggesting appealing POIs along a route, our recommender filters a set of POIs by selecting those that are aligned to the user and the context. Given that the domain of POIs is not as large as journey plans we adopted a collaborative-filtering approach, which has proven to be effective and requires less information about items (POIs in this case). Nevertheless, collaborative-filtering can suffer from data sparsity, thus we chose a Matrix Factorization algorithm to find latent factors and reduce this issue. For both algorithms, their learning process and resulting user models share the same input information:

- The situational data, which includes all the wide range of contextual information occurring in the city (*e.g.*, weather, pollution, crowdedness).
- The history of previous recommendations, that is journey plans and POIs suggested, along the user's context (*e.g.*, purpose and companionship).
- The feedback given by the user about the suggested items (plans or POIs).
- The User profile, to retrieve user's preferences for bootstrapping purposes.

For each user, different user models are learnt according to the set of contexts that are more significant or allow distinguishing better what the user likes most when travelling. Then, when new recommnendations are needed, our system picks the user model that better fits the current context and uses it to either predict user's preference towards a journey plan or select the most appealing POIs that s/he may like to know while travelling. The SUPERHUB recommender employs state-of-the-art approaches to context-aware recommendation that have been demostrated to be especially effective in the tourism domain like the one presented in [3], which considerably enhances the precision of recommendations compared to a state-of-the-art (context-free) recommender.

The term Point of Interest is commonly used in mobility and geographical domains to any relevant geographical location that has some significance (*e.g.*, a building or an important sightseeing location). In the context of IMR the term is used to refer to venues and relevant locations. The SUPERHUB recommender, by following approaches for context-aware recommendation [3], allows improving results and dynamically adapting to the real situation in the city and to users' needs, goals and current context (*e.g.*, in a rush, going to work, with children). In order to do so, it intensively mines the contextual information generated by the Semantic Interpreter to pre-filter user models and to learn and exploit contextual user models. This contextual information is obtained from the semantically-annotated situational data obtained from the processes described in §3. This means that the training process of each recommender computes a user model for each kind of context (*e.g.*, raining, raining and night, sunny). These models are learnt offline, since computing all of them require a significant amount of time. Using this approach, having all the user models of a given user pre-calculated allows improving scalability of the recommending process.

4.1 Journey Plan Recommender

The JPR predicts user score towards Journey Plans or Legs; ideally, there is a large amount of possible Journey Plans or Legs. This implies that any feedback retrieved from users may be too sparse, which makes difficult to find similar users to proceed with a collaborative-filtering approach (*e.g.*, only users that perform the same routes would be found as similar users).

This fact suggests that the best solution to design JPR is choosing a content-based approach, which is consistent with current state of the art on mobility recommenders.

By means of extracting features that define a Journey Plan or Leg, it is possible to learn the preference towards each feature from users feedback given to previous Journey Plans/Legs. For instance, a user may provide positive feedback towards Journey Plans that require little walking and mainly use the bus at night, and negative feedback to Journey Plans that require walking or riding a bike also when it is dark. Thus, JPM can predict better score to Journey Plans that include taking the bus when night rather than walking.

It is worth noticing that user may have explicited the preference towards riding a bike or a bus, but the user model has learnt the preference about the same modes of transport under different contexts. Thus, the training process incorporates users preferences as a starting point and process feedback from previous Journey Plans done to refine those preferences.

4.2 Opportunistic Recommender

The Opportunistic Recommender filters a set of POIs by selecting those that are more appealing to the user. Then, these POIs are added to the Journey Plan to enhance it. Given that the domain of POIs is not as large as Journey Plans it is feasible to consider collaborative-filtering approach, which has proven to be effective and requires less information about items (venues in this case). Nevertheless, collaborative-filtering can suffer from data sparsity, thus it is proposed to use Matrix Factorization to find latent factors and reduce this issue.

5   Conclusions

The approach proposed in this paper is to use a combination of sentiment analysis, semantic inference, information diffusion and big data techniques on top of interactions of users in certain social networks, combined with city-specific knowledge, city events calendars and geospatial data. Data is analysed in two stages, on-line and off-line, in order to learn behavioural patterns and capture those deviations that may reflect events that affect urban mobility. The Semantic Interpreter is currently running and producing results for Barcelona, Milan and Helsinki, the three trials cities for the SUPERHUB project evaluation, plus Mexico DF and Rio de Janeiro as cities with very high amounts of social network inputs. By using an execution mechanism inspired by agent paradigms we make sure that the system is self-dependant and reliable enough to automatically build crowdedness models with data as volatile as social network inputs.

Depending on the periodicity of the aggregation set in the configuration of the Semantic Interpreter instance, the delay between the start of the event in the city and the instant at which it is detected by the SUPERHUB platform may vary, but we have empirically proven it can be as low as 5 minutes. Considering that, according to policy makers from the city of Barcelona, the standard resolution of city-event detection is 15 minutes, this is a relevant result.

Additionally, we propose to take advantage of the mobile app by enabling it with a local semantic interpretation process providing an immediate associated functionality: enhancing the reporting of disruptive events by proactively suggesting events happening nearby the user and presenting the option to confirm or deny them, or to tag them. In this way, users would be generators not only of geolocated data, but also of first-person knowledge of their surrounding context.

Similar proposals have recently appeared that cover some of the aspects of such a system, either from the individual sensoring perspective, closer to multi-agent based systems [6] or from big data techniques applied to social network streams by combining statistical analysis with semantic interpretation [7]. However, such proposals work at a granularity level that is either too high or too low: in the former approach there is, in principle, no centralised mechanism to maintain global aggregations; in the latter, systems do not take advantage of the end-user terminals and their potential dispersion in time and space. In this paper we present a system that can work at both levels, leveraging global aggregations with local awareness to have the best possible picture of the context of the city whenever possible.

Finally, the SUPERHUB recommender, by having a strong focus on the use of semantically-enhanced contextual information, provides novelty to the state of the art beyond the use of recommenders in the mobility domain.

Acknowledgements. This work is supported by the European Project ICT-FP7-289067 SUPERHUB.

References

1. Boccaletti, S., Latora, V., Moreno, Y., Chavez, M.,, D.: HWANG. Complex networks: Structure and dynamics. Physics Reports 424(4-5), 175–308 (2006)
2. Carreras, I., Gabrielli, S., Miorandi, D., Tamilin, A., Cartolano, F., Jakob, M., Marzorati, S.: SUPERHUB: A user-centric perspective on sustainable urban mobility. In: Sense Transport 2012: Proc. of the 6th ACM Workshop on Next Generation Mobile Computing for Dynamic Personalised Travel Planning. ACM (June 2012)
3. Codina, V., Ricci, F., Ceccaroni, L.: Local Context Modeling with Semantic Pre-filtering. In: Proceedings of the 7th ACM Conference on Recommender Systems, pp. 363–366. ACM, New York (2013)
4. Cretti, S., Facca, F.: D2.1 FP7-ICT-2011-7 SUPERHUB - Report on the architecture definition Open Source strategy and adoption pattern. Technical report (March 2012)
5. Diaspero, C., Heinisch, A., Petrova, A.: A Mobile Recommender System for Hiking Walkways (2011)
6. Ellul, C., Gupta, S., Haklay, M.M., Bryson, K.: A Platform for Location Based App Development for Citizen Science and Community Mapping. In: Progress in Location-Based Services, pp. 71–90. Springer, Heidelberg (2013)
7. Gabrielli, L., Rinzivillo, S., Ronzano, F., Villatoro, D.: From Tweets to Semantic Trajectories: Mining Anomalous Urban Mobility Patterns. In: Nin, J., Villatoro, D. (eds.) CitiSens 2013. LNCS (LNAI), vol. 8313, pp. 26–35. Springer, Heidelberg (2014)

8. Garcia-Gasulla, D., Tejeda-Gómez, A., Alvarez-Napagao, S., Oliva-Felipe, L., Vázquez-Salceda, J.: Detection of events through collaborative social network data. In: Proceedings of the 6th International Workshop on Emergent Intelligence on Networked Agents (WEIN 2014) (May 2014)
9. Gomez, J.T., Marrè, M.S., Serra, J.P.: tweetStimuli: Discovering social structure of influence (2012)
10. Hickey, R.: The Clojure programming language. In: DLS 2008: Proceedings of the 2008 Symposium on Dynamic Languages. ACM (July 2008)
11. Knoch, S., Chapko, A., Emrich, A., Werth, D., Loos, P.: A Context-Aware Running Route Recommender Learning from User Histories Using Artificial Neural Networks. In: 2012 23rd International Workshop on Database and Expert Systems Applications (DEXA), pp. 106–110 (2012)
12. McGinty, L., Smyth, B.: Personalised Route Planning: A Case-Based Approach. In: Blanzieri, E., Portinale, L. (eds.) EWCBR 2000. LNCS (LNAI), vol. 1898, pp. 431–443. Springer, Heidelberg (2000)
13. Ricci, F.: Travel recommender systems. IEEE Intelligent Systems (2002)
14. Srivastava, M., Abdelzaher, T., Szymanski, B.: Human-centric sensing. Philosophical Transactions of the Royal Society A: Mathematical, Physical and Engineering Sciences 370, 176–197 (1958, 2011)
15. Weng, J., Lee, B.S.: Event Detection in Twitter. In: ICWSM (2011)

Mining Social Interaction Data in Virtual Worlds

Syed Fahad Allam Shah[1] and Gita Sukthankar[2]

[1] Microsoft Corporation, Bellevue, WA, USA
fashah@microsoft.com
[2] University of Central Florida, Orlando, FL, USA
gitars@eecs.ucf.edu

Abstract. Virtual worlds and massively multi-player online games are rich sources of information about large-scale teams and groups, offering the tantalizing possibility of harvesting data about group formation, social networks, and network evolution. However these environments lack many of the cues that facilitate natural language processing in other conversational settings and different types of social media. Public chat data often features players who speak simultaneously, use jargon and emoticons, and only erratically adhere to conversational norms. This chapter presents techniques for inferring the existence of social links from unstructured conversational data collected from groups of participants in the Second Life virtual world.

Keywords: Network Text Analysis, Longitudinal Analysis, Virtual Worlds, Community Detection.

1 Introduction

Massively multi-player online games (MMOGs) and virtual environments provide new outlets for human social interaction that are significantly different from both face-to-face interactions and non-physically-embodied social networking tools such as Facebook and Twitter. We aim to study group dynamics in these virtual worlds by collecting and analyzing public conversational patterns of Second Life users.

Second Life (SL) is a massively multi-player online environment that allows users to construct and inhabit their own 3D world. In Second Life, users control avatars, through which they are able to explore different environments and interact with other avatars in a variety of ways. One of the most commonly used methods of interaction in Second Life is basic text chat. Users are able to chat with other users directly through private instant messages (IMs) or to broadcast chat messages to all avatars within a given radius of their avatar using a public chat channel.

The physical environment in Second Life is laid out in a 2D arrangement, known as the SLGrid. The SLGrid is comprised of many regions, with each region hosted on its own server and offering a fully featured 3D environment shaped by the user population. The total number of SL users is approximately 16 million, with a weekly user login activity reported in the vicinity of 0.5 million [26]. Second Life contains users of widely divergent expertise levels, ranging from complete novices who congregate in the orientation areas practicing basic controls to highly skilled scripters who craft objects

F. Koch et al. (Eds.): CARE/AVSA 2014, CCIS 498, pp. 86–105, 2015.

and storefronts to sell within Second Life. There is a broad spectrum of group persistence. One can observe rapidly-formed crowds gathered around a temporary attraction, and also semi-permanent groups of people who share interests either within or outside of the virtual environment. Similar to real-life, these differences are somewhat correlated with SL regions, since each SL region contains a different mix of entertainment opportunities.

Although Second Life provides us with rich opportunities to observe the public behavior of large groups of users, it is difficult to interpret who the users are communicating to and what they are trying to say from public chat data. Network text analysis systems such as Automap [3] that incorporate linguistic analysis techniques such as stemming, named-entity recognition, and n-gram identification are not effective on this data since many of the linguistic pre-processing steps are defeated by the slang and rapid topic shifts of the Second Life users. This is a hard problem even for human observers and it was impossible for us to unambiguously identify the recipient of many of the utterances in our dataset. In this article, we present an algorithm for addressing this problem, Shallow Semantic Temporal Overlap (SSTO) [27], that combines temporal and language information to infer the existence of directional links between participants. One of the problems is that using temporal overlap as a cue for detecting links can produce extraneous links and low precision. To reduce these extraneous links, we propose the use of community detection. Optimizing network modularity reduces the number of extraneous links generated by overly generous temporal co-occurrence assumption but does not significantly improve the performance of SSTO.

There has been increasing interest in mining community structure in these networks. In general, network sections exhibiting denser linkages among themselves are classified as part of the same community. This phenomena has been studied in social networks, biochemical networks and the WWW [23,11,9,13,5]. Understanding the community structure of a network can reveal interesting trends and increase our knowledge of the function and evolution of the system.

To examine the influence of the extracted groups found with community detection on network evolution, we analyze the system using the dynamic actor-oriented model for network evolution [32]. We use this model to explore the evolution of the network (mined from the dialog exchanges) considering the community membership from previous time period as an actor attribute. This gives us statistical evidence whether the community membership persists over time and provides additional support on the accuracy of our community detection. Using longitudinal network data analysis [33], we consider sequences of network observations extracted from dialog exchanges, along with attributes of the SL avatars, and model them in an actor-oriented model using RSiena (Simulation Investigation for Empirical Network Analysis) [35]. The methodology has been successfully employed in a number of sociological studies on the influences of different factors on group behavior [18,24,8,14,16].

2 Prior Work

Second Life is a unique test bed for research studies, allowing scientists to study a broad range of human behaviors. For instance, social scientists have used Second Life to study norms and etiquette in dressing and meeting people [7]. Several studies on user interaction in virtual environments have been conducted in SL including studies on conversation [37] and virtual agents [2]. Zhao and Wang describe a technique for simulating multiple agents in a virtual environment using a hierarchical model of cognition and decision making [39]. Second Life has also been used to recreate many real-world environments. Physical versions of libraries, art galleries, universities, and corporate meeting facilities have been developed for SL to serve as virtual portals for meetings and information access.

In this chapter, we address the problem of constructing social network linkages from public chat exchanges. This is simultaneously useful for analyzing the group dynamics in different Second Life regions and has the potential practical benefit of allowing Second Life land owners to analyze the relative utility of various attractions. Dialog analysis has been previously explored within the Restaurant Game [22], where a corpus of human dialog is collected and leveraged to improve the realism of the bot's dialog in a social situation. There has been research on the problem of constructing social networks of MMOG players, for example, Shi and Huang [30] demonstrate that concepts from social network analysis and data mining can be used identify MMOG tasks. In this article our social network analysis is focused toward revealing network characteristics rather than actor characteristics, which is significantly different from prior work at mining social networks from multi-player game data. We wish to identify differences between *groups* of participants rather than between different *actors* within the same social network. Communities within USENET have been analyzed by comparing structures of induced social networks for each group using metrics such as size, degree, and reciprocity [17]. Our analysis of Second Life communities is similar in concept but uses different techniques for constructing linkages. Kahanda and Neville [15] have compared the relative utility of different types of features at predicting friendship links in social networks; in this study we examine direct conversational data and do not attempt to predict unobserved links based on other types of events.

The problem of analyzing environmental effects on groups of users has been explored in other types of social media. Hogg and Lerman [12] describe a general stochastic process-based approach to modeling user-contributory web sites in an attempt to analyze how the design of the website affects user behavior. Fisher et al. [4] perform community analysis from the organizer's point of view and address problems such as assessing the value of online community and monitoring social activity within space. Our work can be seen as a similar effort in virtual worlds where owners are interested in attracting users, performing usage analysis and learning user activity models.

Although Second Life provides us with rich opportunities to observe the public behavior of large groups of users, it is difficult for even humans to identify who a user is communicating with at a given moment; for instance, it was impossible for us to unambiguously identify the target for many of the utterances in our dataset even with human labelers. Much of the previous work on analyzing chat has been restricted to a small number of users and is topic-specific. One notable exception is the work by the Naval Postgraduate School on collecting and analyzing the NPS corpus [6], which is based on chat dialogs from online chat rooms. Using a combination of manual annotations and filtering techniques, Wu et al. [38] divide the utterances into semantic classes; in contrast we use semantic cues to identify social connections. Compared to our SL dataset, the NPS corpus contains more discussion about the participants' real-life interactions whereas the SL data is more heavily slanted toward discussions of the virtual world (e.g., scripting, shopping). The NPS corpus has additionally been used in a study of topic identification [1], which is something that we hope to do in future work.

Another similar effort done within a controlled environment on a smaller corpus is that of [29]. They employed manual annotation at four levels: communication links, dialog acts, local topics and meso-topics, whereas in our case we are concerned with the automation of the first level (communication links). Another important difference is that they imposed structure to their communications by directing the conversation towards a topic and using an arbiter. Our dataset is unique in its size, lack of communication structure, and dynamic groups.

3 Approach

To conduct our study of group social interactions in Second Life, we had to address the following issues:

1. partitioning unstructured dialog into separate conversations;
2. identifying links from the partitioned data;
3. performing longitudinal network data analysis to validate communities.

Figure 1 shows the overall data collection architecture. Multiple bots, stationed in different SL regions, listen to all the messages within their hearing range on the public channel. The bots forward chat messages to the server, which parses and conditions messages for storage in the dialog database. Occasionally the server sends the bots navigational commands and optional dialog response if the communication was directed to the bot. Linkages between SL actors are inferred offline by partitioning the unstructured data into separate conversations; these linkages are used to construct the graphs used in the social network analysis.

3.1 Bot Construction

Instead of being controlled by a human user, Second Life avatars can be controlled by an automated agent known as a bot. A bot connects to the SLGrid like a normal user, but is controlled by a program that does not require user interaction. Our bots were implemented using LibOpenMetaverse (LibOMV) [21], an open source .NET based library that allows applications to be able to simulate much of the functionality of the official Second Life client software. Using this library, we were able to build multiple bots that log in at a given location and collect all desired data for chat messages within the bot's hearing range on the public channel.

The bot application begins execution by passing login info for a Second Life account to LibOMV. Once LibOMV successfully logs into Second Life, the application enters its main execution loop. Here, the application waits for notification from LibOMV that an event has occurred involving the bot. When a chat message is received, LibOMV passes the following information to the application: the name of the user who sent the message, the time and date the message was received, the region and local coordinates

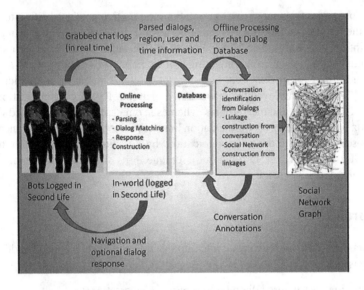

Parsed dialogs,
Grabbed chat logs   region, user and   Offline Processing
(in real time)   time information   for chat Dialog
Database

Online   Database   -Conversation
Processing   identification
from Dialogs
- Parsing   - Linkage
- Dialog Matching   construction from
- Response   conversation
Construction   -Social Network
construction from
linkages

Bots Logged in   In-world (logged
Second Life   in Second Life)   Social
Network
Conversation   Graph
Annotations

Navigation and
optional dialog
response

Fig. 1. Multi-agent architecture for Second Life data collection

(relative to the bot's current region) that the message was sent from, and the text of the message itself. After this information is recorded in the database, the application returns to the main loop, waiting for the next event to occur. Figure 2 shows a bot harvesting data in Second Life.

3.2 Data Collection

We obtained conversation data from eight different regions in Second Life over fourteen days of data collection; the reader is referred to [28] for details. To study user dialogs, we examined daily and hourly data for five randomly selected days in the eight regions. In total, the dataset contains 523 hours of information over the five days (80,000 utterances) considered for the analysis across all regions. We did a hand-annotation of one hour of data from each of the regions to serve as a basis for comparison. Table 1 gives an example of dialog exchanged between users in the RezzMe region.

Second Life's multi-user, open-ended setting poses unique challenges to dialog analysis. In such situations it is imperative to identify conversational connections before proceeding to higher level analysis like topic modeling, which is itself a challenging problem. We considered several approaches to analyzing our dialog dataset, ranging from statistical NLP approaches using classifiers to corpus-based approaches using tagger/parsers; however we discovered that there is no corpus available for group-based online chat in an open-ended dialog setting. It is challenging to label the conversations themselves for the large size of the dataset and the ambiguity in a multi-user open-ended setting makes it difficult even for a human to figure who is talking to whom. Furthermore, the variability of the utterances and the nuances such as emoticons, abbreviations and the presence of emphasizers in spellings (e.g., "Yayyy") makes it difficult to train appropriate classifiers. As for the parser/tagger-based approaches, since there is no

Fig. 2. Bot collecting public chat messages

Table 1. Anonymized transcript of a public conversation collected in Second Life's RezzMe region

User Name	Dialog
user1	anyone know if there's a way to turn off notifications in local chat for shields or any other objects when you're in a no-rez zone?
user2	brb need to get drink :)
user3	lol I put the pengiun in the trash can
user4	not too many who knows what it actually stands for
user5	user1, pls can you explain in more detail what you ask? mute it?
user3	GRR YOU DARN PENGUIN
user4	/status
user1	i can paste it in for you:
user5	user3 pls dont pushy ppl
user3	ok sorry
user1	Can't rez object 'animcept4' at {55.9452, 35.1487, 23.4774 } on parcel 'Help People Island'! in region Help People Island because the owner of this land does not allow it Use the land tool to see land restrictions

corpus available and the vocabulary is not restricted to English words, the parser/tagger performs poorly.

Consequently, we decided to investigate approaches that utilize non linguistic cues such as temporal co-occurrence. Although temporal co-occurrence can create a large number of false links, many aspects of the network group structure are preserved. Hence we opted to implement two-pass approach: 1) create a noisy network based solely on temporal co-occurrence 2) perform modularity detection on the network to detect communities of users 3) attempt to filter extraneous links using the results of the community detection.

3.3 Modularity Optimization

In prior work, community membership has been successfully used to identify latent dimensions in social networks [36] using techniques such as eigenvector-based modularity optimization [20] which allows for both complete and partial memberships. As described in [20], modularity (denoted by Q below) measures the chances of seeing a node in the network versus its occurrence being completely random; it can be defined as the sum of the random chance $A_{ij} - \frac{k_i k_j}{2m}$ (where A_{ij} is the entry from adjacency matrix, k_i the node's degree, and $m = \frac{1}{2}\sum_i k_i$ the total edges in the network) summed over all pairs of vertices i, j, where s equals 1 if a vertex falls in community 1 and -1 if it falls in community 2:

$$Q = \frac{1}{4m} \sum_{ij} \left[A_{ij} - \frac{k_i k_j}{2m} \right] s_i s_j \tag{1}$$

If B is defined as the modularity matrix given by $A_{ij} - \frac{k_i k_j}{2m}$, which is a real symmetric matrix and s column vectors whose elements are s_i then Equation 1 can be written as $Q = \frac{1}{4m} \sum_{i=1}^{n} (u_i^T s)^2 \beta_i$, where β_i is the eigenvalue of B corresponding to the eigenvector u (u_i are the normalized eigenvectors of B so that $s = \sum_i^n a_i u_i$ and $a_i = u_i^T s$). We use the leading eigenvector approach to spectral optimization of modularity as described in [19] for the strict community partitioning (s being 1 or -1 and not continuous). For the maximum positive eigenvalue we set $s = 1$ for the corresponding element of the eigenvector if it is positive and negative otherwise. Finally we repeatedly partition a group of size n_g in two and calculate the change in modularity measure given by $\Delta q = \frac{1}{4m} \sum_{l=1}^{c} \sum_{i,j \in g} [B_{ij} - \delta_{ij} \sum_{k \in g} B_{ik}] s_{il} s_{jl}$, where l is the number of communities from 1 to c and δ_{ij} is the Kronecker δ symbol, terminating if the change is not positive and otherwise choosing the sign of s (the partition) in the same way as described earlier.

3.4 Shallow Semantics and Temporal Overlap Algorithm (SSTO)

Because of an inability to use statistical machine learning approaches due to the lack of sufficiently labeled data and absence of a tagger/parser that can interpret chat dialog data, we developed a rule-based algorithm that relies on shallow semantic analysis of linguistic cues that commonly occur in chat data including mentions of named entities as well as the temporal co-occurrence of utterances to generate a to/from labeling for the chat dialogs with directed links between users. Our algorithm employs the following types of rules:

salutations: Salutations are frequent and can be identified using keywords such as "hi", "hello", "hey". The initial speaker is marked as the *from* user and users that respond within a designated temporal window are labeled as *to* users.

questions: Question words (e.g., "who", "what", "how") are treated in the same way as salutations. We apply the same logic to requests for help (which are often marked by words such as "can", "would").

usernames: When a dialog begins or ends with all or part of a username (observed during the analysis period), the username is marked as *to*, and the speaker marked as *from*.

second person pronouns: If the dialog begins with a second person pronoun (i.e., "you", "your"), then the previous speaker is considered as the *from* user and the current speaker the *to* user; explicit mentions of a username override this.

temporal co-occurrences: Our system includes rules for linking users based on temporal co-occurrence of utterances. These rules are triggered by a running conversation of 8–12 utterances.

This straightforward algorithm is able to capture sufficient information from the dialogs and is comparable in performance to SSTO with community information, as discussed below.

3.5   Temporal Overlap Algorithm

The temporal overlap algorithm consists of using the temporal co-occurrence to construct the links. It exploits the default timeout in Second Life (20 minutes) and performs a lookup for 20 minutes beginning from the occurrence of a given username and constructs an undirected link between the speakers and this user. This process is repeated for all users within that time window (one hour or day) in 20 minute periods. This algorithm gives a candidate pool of initial links between the users without considering any semantic information. Later, we show that incorporating community information from any source (similar time overlap or SSTO based) and on any scale (daily or hourly) enables us to effectively prune links, showing the efficacy of mining community membership information.

3.6   Incorporating Community Membership

The dataset was separated from daily logs into hourly partitions, based on the belief that an hour is a reasonable duration for social interactions in a virtual world. The hourly partitioned data for each day is used to generate user graph adjacency matrices using the two algorithms described earlier (Sections 3.4 and 3.5). The adjacency matrix is then used to generate the spectral partitions for the communities in the graph, which are then used to back annotate the tables containing the to/from labeling (in the case of the SSTO algorithm). These annotations serve as an additional cue capturing community membership. Not all the matrices are decomposable into smaller communities so we treat such graphs of users as a single community.

There are multiple options for using the community information: it can be calculated on an hourly or daily basis, using the initial run from either SSTO or the temporal overlap algorithms. The daily data is a long-term view that focuses on the stable network of users while the hourly labeling is a fine-grained view that can enable the study of how the social communities evolve over time. The SSTO algorithm gives us a conservative set of directed links between users while the temporal overlap algorithm provides a more inclusive hypothesis of users connected by undirected links.

For the SSTO algorithm, we consider several variants of using the community information:

SSTO: Raw SSTO without community information;
SSTO+LC: SSTO (with loose community information) relies on community information from the previous run only when we fail to make a link using language cues;
SSTO+SC: SSTO (with strict community information) always uses language cues in conjunction with the community information.

For the temporal overlap algorithms, we use the community information from the previous run.

TO: Raw temporal overlap algorithm without community information;
TO+DT: Temporal overlap plus daily community information;
TO+HT: Temporal overlap plus hourly community information.

4 Results

In this section we summarize the results from a comparison of the social networks constructed from the different algorithms. While comparing networks for similarity is a difficult problem [25], we restrict our attention to comparing networks as a whole in terms of the link difference (using Frobenius norm) and a one-to-one comparison for the *to* and *from* labelings for each dialog on the ground-truthed subset (using precision and recall).

4.1 Network Comparison Using the Frobenius Norm

We constructed a gold-standard subset of the data by hand-annotating the to/from fields for a randomly-selected hour from each of the Second Life regions. It is to be noted that there were instances where even a human was unable to determine the person addressed due to the complex overlapping nature of the dialogs in group conversation in an open ended setting (Table 3).

To compare the generated networks against this baseline, we use two approaches. First we compute a Frobenius norm [10] for the adjacency matrices from the corresponding networks. The Frobenius norm is the matrix norm of an $M \times N$ matrix A and is defined as:

$$\|A\| = \sqrt{\sum_{i=1}^{M} \sum_{j=1}^{N} |a_{ij}|^2}. \tag{2}$$

The Frobenius norm directly measures whether the two networks have the same links and can be used since the networks consists of the same nodes (users). Thus, the norm serves as a measure of error (a perfect match would result in a norm of 0). Table 4.1 shows the results from this analysis.

Table 2. Frobenius norm: comparison against hand-annotated subset

	SSTO	SSTO+LC	SSTO+SC	TO	TO+DT	TO+HT
Help Island Public	35.60	41.19	46.22	224.87	162.00	130.08
Help People Island	62.23	60.50	66.34	20.29	20.29	54.88
Mauve	48.45	45.11	51.91	58.44	58.44	49.89
Morris	24.67	18.92	20.76	43.12	37.54	38.98
Kuula	32.12	30.75	32.66	83.22	73.15	77.82
Pondi Beach	20.63	21.77	21.56	75.07	62.62	71.02
Moose Beach	17.08	18.30	21.07	67.05	53.64	50.97
Rezz Me	36.70	39.74	45.78	38.72	39.01	41.10
Total error	277.48	**276.28**	306.30	610.78	507.21	514.74

4.2 Direct Label Comparisons

The second quantitative measure we present is the head-to-head comparison of the to/from labelings for the dialogs using any of the approaches described above (for SSTO) against the hand annotated dialogs. This gives us the true positives and false positives for the approaches and allows us to see which one is performing better on the dataset, and if there is an effect in different Second Life regions. Table 3 shows the results from this analysis.

For the temporal overlap algorithm (TO), the addition of the community information reduces the link noise, irrespective of the scale — be it hourly or daily. This is shown by the decreasing value of the Frobenius norm in all the cases as compared to the value obtained using temporal overlap algorithm alone. In general shallow semantic approach (SSTO) performs the best and is only improved slightly by the loose incorporation of community information. For the SSTO algorithm, the daily or hourly community partition also does not affect the improvement. Table 3 shows how the dialog labeling generated from various algorithms agrees with the ground truth notations produced by a human labeler. Since TO only produces undirected links, we do not include it in the comparison. Plain SSTO generally results in a better precision and recall than SSTO plus either strict or loose community labeling. These results are also confirmed from the visualizations for one of the hours of data for all the three methods in figure 3, where the SSTO network most closely resembles the hand-labeled network while the TO network contains many spurious links.

The challenging nature of this dataset is evident in the overall low precision and recall scores, not only for the proposed algorithms but also for human labelers. We attribute this largely to the inherent ambiguity in the observed utterances. Among the techniques, SSTO performs best, confirming that leveraging semantics is more useful than merely observing temporal co occurrence. We observe that community information is not reliably informative for SSTO but does help TO, showing that link pruning through network structure is useful in the absence of semantic information.

Table 3. Precision/Recall values for one-to-one labeling comparison

		Help Island Public	Help People Island	Mauve	Morris	Kuula	Pondi Beach	Moose Beach	Rezz Me
Total Dialogs		360	184	128	179	227	144	128	97
Hand	recall	0.6278	0.9076	0.9453	0.6983	0.8370	0.6944	0.6797	0.8866
Labeled	total	226	167	121	125	190	100	87	86
SSTO+SC	match	61	59	49	43	63	27	12	23
	precision	0.2607	0.6629	0.6364	0.4216	0.4632	0.3971	0.2105	0.4600
	recall	0.2699	0.3533	0.4050	0.3440	0.3316	0.2700	0.1379	0.2674
	F-Score	0.2652	0.4609	0.4204	0.3789	0.3865	0.3214	0.1667	0.3382
	total	234	89	77	102	136	68	57	50
SSTO+LC	match	61	51	37	39	52	26	12	15
	precision	0.3005	0.6456	0.6607	0.4643	0.4561	0.4194	0.2667	0.4688
	recall	0.2699	0.3054	0.3058	0.3120	0.2737	0.2600	0.1379	0.1744
	F-Score	0.2844	0.4146	0.4181	0.3732	0.3421	0.3210	0.1818	0.2542
	total	203	79	56	84	114	62	45	32
SSTO	match	76	68	51	45	66	30	20	27
	precision	0.3065	0.7083	0.6145	0.4500	0.4748	0.4225	0.3077	0.4576
	recall	0.3363	0.4072	0.4215	0.3600	0.3474	0.3000	0.2299	0.3140
	F-Score	0.3207	0.5171	0.5000	0.3617	0.4012	0.3509	0.2299	0.3724
	total	248	96	83	100	139	71	65	59

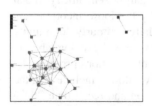 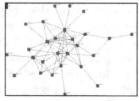 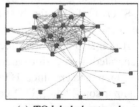

(a) Hand labeled network.   (b) SSTO labeled network.   (c) TO labeled network.

Fig. 3. Networks from different algorithms for one hour in the Help Island Public region

5   Evaluating Community Persistence

To evaluate the usefulness of the community detection and determine if the patterns determined by the algorithm prevail over time, we devised the following experiment utilizing the longitudinal (cross-sectional) analysis of the network in relation to the attribute information:

1. We use social networks formed from three days of data and determine the community membership for each of the actors in this set.
2. Next, we randomly select four hours worth of data from a subsequent day to be used for longitudinal analysis.

3. We use the community membership information as a constant actor-covariate. The objective here was to explore if the actors with same community membership communicate more frequently among themselves across multiple days, hence testifying to the stability of the communities and our SSTO link-mining algorithm.

There were total 98 actors across the selected four hours period; 47 actors are common across all four days of data. We use the stochastic actor-oriented model from Snijders [34,33] to explore the co-evolution of the network behavior including the parameters for Similarity (to evaluate the hypothesis of preferential communication between actors of the same community), Ego (covariate-related activity), and Alter (covariate-related popularity).

Here we summarize the network evolution model used in RSiena (Simulation Investigation for Empirical Network Analysis) [35]. The network evolution model examines the actors' decisions to establish new ties or break existing ties (as defined by evaluation and endowment functions), and the model of the timing of these decisions (controlled by rate function). The objective function of the actor is then defined by the sum of the network evaluation function and the network endowment function as shown in Equation 3:

$$u^{net}(x) = f^{net}(x) + g^{net}(x). \tag{3}$$

The network evaluation function for actor i can be written as:

$$f^{net}(x) = \sum_k \beta_k^{net} s_{ik}^{net}(x) \tag{4}$$

where β_k^{net} denotes the parameters and $s_{ik}^{net}(x)$ the effects (discussed below).

The structural part of the network dynamics is modeled by the structural effects that depend only on the network. We considered the following two structural effects in our model:

- **out-degree** or **density effect** as given by

$$s_{i1}^{net}(x) = x_{i+} = \sum_j x_{ij} i \tag{5}$$

where the presence of a tie from i to j is indicated by $x_{ij} = 1$ and $x_{ij} = 0$ denotes the absence and
- **reciprocity effect**, defined as the number of reciprocated ties

$$s_{i2}^{net}(x) = \sum_j x_{ij} x_{ji}. \tag{6}$$

Covariates are the variables that depend on the actors (also called actor covariates). For actor-dependent covariates v_j the following effects were used for the analysis:

- **covariate-alter** or **covariate-related popularity** is the sum of the covariate over all actors with which actor i has a tie and is given by:

$$s_{i3}^{net}(x) = \sum_j x_{ij} v_j. \tag{7}$$

– **covariate-ego** or **covariate-related activity** is the actor i's out-degree weighted by his covariate value as given by:

$$s_{i4}^{net}(x) = v_i x_{i+}.$$

(8)

– **covariate-related similarity** is the sum of centered similarity scores sim_{ij}^v between the actor i and the other actors j that are tied to i as given by:

$$s_{i5}^{net}(x) = \sum_j x_{ij}(\text{sim}_{ij}^v - \hat{\text{sim}}^v)$$

(9)

where $\hat{\text{sim}}^v$ is the mean of all similarity scores given by $\text{sim}_{ij}^v = \frac{\Delta - |v_i - v_j|}{\Delta}$ and $\Delta = \max_{ij} |v_i - v_j|$ is the observed range of the covariate v.

The network rate function λ^{net} is given by:

$$\lambda_i^{net}(\rho, \alpha, x, m) = \lambda_{i1}^{net} \lambda_{i2}^{net} \lambda_{i3}^{net}$$

(10)

where the factors in Equation 10 depend respectively on period m, actor covariates, and actor position.

The dependence on the period can be denoted by a simple factor given in:

$$\lambda_{i1}^{net} = \rho_m^{net}$$

(11)

for $m = 1, ..., M - 1$. If we have $M = 2$ observations, the basic rate parameter can be written as ρ^{net}. The effect of actor covariates with values v_{hi} can be denoted by a factor as shown:

$$\lambda_{i2}^{net} = \exp\left(\sum_h \alpha_h v_{hi}\right).$$

(12)

The actor's dependence on the position can be modeled as a function of the actor's out-degree, in-degree, number of reciprocated relations, and reciprocated degrees, given by:

$$x_{i+} = \sum_j x_{ij}, x_{+i} = \sum_j x_{ij}, x_{i(r)} = \sum_j x_{ij} x_{ji}$$

(13)

where $x_{ii} = 0$ for all i. The out-degree's contribution to λ_{i3}^{net} is a factor $\exp(\alpha_h x_{i+})$ if the associated parameter is given by α_h for some h, and similarly for the in-degree and the reciprocated degree contributions.

5.1 Actor-Oriented Model

The main component of the actor-oriented model is the evaluation function [33,34], given in Equation 4. The objective function can give an idea of the "attractiveness" of the network for a given actor. Interpretation of the values for the estimates can be helped by the objective function computations that give an idea of how attractive different tie changes are.

A variable V's effects can best be understood by considering all effects in the model on which it appears simultaneously. In our network dynamics model, the ego, alter, and similarity effects of a variable V were considered and the formula for their contribution can be obtained from the components listed in Equation 4 as

$$\beta_{ego} v_i x_{i+} + \beta_{alter} \sum_j x_{ij} v_j + \beta_{sim} \sum_j \left(sim_{ij}^v - \hat{sim}^v \right) \tag{14}$$

where the similarity score is given by $sim_{ij}^v = 1 - \frac{|v_i - v_j|}{\Delta_V}$ with $\Delta_V = \max_{ij} |v_i - v_j|$ denoting the observed range of the covariate v and sim^v being the mean of all similarity scores. Note, for simplicity, the superscript *net* is removed from the notation for the parameters.

The single tie variable x_{ij} gives the contribution of the tie from i to j; hence, the difference between the values of Equation 14 for $x_{ij} = 1$ and $x_{ij} = 0$ can be computed from this equation. Since we are using RSiena which centers the values around the mean, Equation 14 can be rewritten as

$$\beta_{ego} v_i x_{i+} + \beta_{alter} \sum_j x_{ij} v_j + \beta_{sim} \sum_j \left(1 - \frac{|v_i - v_j|}{\Delta_V} - \hat{sim}^v \right) \tag{15}$$

This section details the statistics obtained from running the estimation on the Ego, Alter, and Similarity parameters considered for the three covariates (age, gender, and community).[1] First we present summary statistics for the network as shown in the Table 4. The average density for all the periods is quite low, indicating the sparse nature of the data. The average degree shows that only observation time 1 has an average close to 0.5 while the rest are low indicating the asymmetric nature of the ties. Lastly the number of ties are listed for each, where the higher number of ties in observation time 1 explains its higher density, whereas the missing fraction for all observation times being zero.

Table 4. Network density indicators

Observation Time	1	2	3	4
density	0.006	0.003	0.003	0.003
average degree	0.538	0.286	0.286	0.308
number of ties	49	26	26	28
missing fraction	0.000	0.000	0.000	0.000

Table 5 shows the changes between the observations for each period. There are no changes between periods 1-2 and 2-3 in contrast to the high number of changes from 3-4 (indicated by a higher value of the distance). This indicates that the ties that were observed in observation 1 persist in observation 2, observation 2 ties persist to observation 3, but not so for the observation 4. This might be due to the high influx of users during period 4.

---

[1] In this study, age and gender refer to the avatar's listed age and gender, rather than the player demographics, which are not publicly available.

Table 5. Changes between observations

Periods	0 to 0	0 to 1	1 to 0	1 to 1	Distance	Jaccard	Missing
1 to 2	8115	26	49	0	0	0.000	0 (0%)
2 to 3	8138	26	26	0	0	0.000	0 (0%)
3 to 4	8139	25	23	3	27	0.059	0 (0%)

5.2   Estimation Procedure

We used the Method of Moments (MoM) [31,34], where the parameters are estimated in such a way that expected values of a vector of selected statistics are equal to their observed values for the network. The SIENA software implements two methods for MoM estimation: conditional and unconditional. The difference between the two is in the stopping criteria for the simulations of the network evolution.

For unconditional estimation, the network evolution simulations for each time period continue until a predetermined time (taken to be 1.0 for each consecutive time period) has passed. In conditional estimation, the simulations for each period continue to run until a stopping criterion (calculated from the observed data) is reached. It is possible to do conditioning for each of the dependent variables. The conditioning on the network variable refers to running the simulations until the difference in entries for the initially observed network of this period and the simulated network equals the number of entries in the adjacency matrix for the difference between the initial and the final networks of this period. We used the conditional MoM for the community and age covariates and unconditional MoM for gender covariate.

5.3   Convergence Check

A convergence check can be computed from the deviations between the simulated values of the statistics and the observed values. Ideally these deviations should be as close to zero as possible for good convergence. Siena provides t-statistics computed from these averages and standard deviations. The recommendation for the t-statistics for the longitudinal analysis [35] is that the convergence is excellent when these values are less than 0.1 (absolute value), good when less than 0.2, and moderate when less than 0.3. In our case the t-ratios for all estimated parameters in the model were less than 0.1 in the absolute indicating good convergence.

5.4   Interpretation of Parameter Values

The rate parameter (ρ) for the three periods is shown in the Table 6. A value of near zero for the first two periods (1 and 2) indicates that there is very little change between these two periods, while a value of 3.25 indicates the estimated number of changes per actor between the two observations comes out to be approximately 3 ties. It is to be noted that this refers to unobserved changes, and that some of these changes may cancel, such that the average observed number of differences per actor can be actually smaller than the estimated number of unobserved changes.

Table 6. Rate parameter estimates

Rate Parameter	Estimate	Standard Error
Period 1	0.0247	0.0242
Period 2	0.0476	0.0508
Period 3	3.2528	0.8116

We also included outdegree (density), however as the [35] points out, no definite conclusion can be made on the basis of this value alone as all the parameters depend on this parameter. It has a near constant value of -1.9304 across all our estimates.

We explored three constant actor covariates in our model: 1) community membership 2) Second Life avatar gender 3) Second Life avatar age (number of days the avatar has existed). The values for the Ego, Alter and Similarity for the three actor covariates are presented in Table 7. A positive value of similarity indicates that for the covariate the actors are more likely to make connection to other actors of the same value of the covariate as them, whereas a negative value indicates otherwise. The following can be concluded from the values for similarity in Table 7.

1. A high positive value of similarity for community means that more actors are likely to connect to other actors that have same value of community membership. This supports our hypothesis about the value of our community detection procedure.
2. A slight positive value of similarity for the gender means that actors are more likely to talk to other people that are of the same SL avatar gender.
3. A negative value of similarity for SL age means that actors are more likely to communicate to other actors that are different from their own age group.

Table 7. Similarity estimates for the constant covariates

Parameter	Community	Gender	Age
Ego	-0.3770 (0.3300)	-0.0350 (0.5568)	0.0379 (0.6681)
Alter	-1.4736 (0.5547)	-0.0350 (0.5568)	-0.7767 (0.5726)
Similarity	3.8121 (3.4156)	0.4057 (0.5131)	-1.1280 (3.3675)

5.5 Model Estimates for the Community Covariate

In Section 5.4 we discussed the values for the similarity, ego and alter covariates given in the Table 7 for the three covariates (age, gender and community) and their effect on the tendency of the actors to form links. The community covariate ranges from 0-13 (values 10 and 11 were not used as they represent structural zeros and ones respectively within RSiena), with average value $\bar{v} = 1.857$ and average dyadic similarity $\hat{sim}^v = 0.8037$. Substituting these values into Equation 15 yields Equation 16 and Table 8 gives the values from the equation for each value of v_i, v_j for the covariate.

$$-0.38(v_i - \bar{v}) - 0.12(v_j - \bar{v}) + 3.81\left(1 - \frac{|v_i - v_j|}{\Delta_V} - 0.8037\right) \qquad (16)$$

Table 8. Contribution from ego, alter and similarity for the community covariate

v_i/v_j	0	1	2	3	4	5	6	7	8	9	12	13
0	1.68	1.56	1.44	1.32	1.2	1.08	0.96	0.84	0.72	0.6	0.24	0.12
1	1.3	1.18	1.06	0.94	0.82	0.7	0.58	0.46	0.34	0.22	-0.14	-0.26
2	0.92	0.8	0.68	0.56	0.44	0.32	0.2	0.08	-0.04	-0.16	-0.52	-0.64
3	0.54	0.42	0.3	0.18	0.06	-0.06	-0.18	-0.3	-0.42	-0.54	-0.9	-1.02
4	0.16	0.04	-0.08	-0.2	-0.32	-0.44	-0.56	-0.68	-0.8	-0.92	-1.28	-1.4
5	-0.22	-0.34	-0.46	-0.58	-0.7	-0.82	-0.94	-1.06	-1.18	-1.3	-1.66	-1.78
6	-0.6	-0.72	-0.84	-0.96	-1.08	-1.2	-1.32	-1.44	-1.56	-1.68	-2.04	-2.16
7	-0.98	-1.1	-1.22	-1.34	-1.46	-1.58	-1.7	-1.82	-1.94	-2.06	-2.42	-2.54
8	-1.36	-1.48	-1.6	-1.72	-1.84	-1.96	-2.08	-2.2	-2.32	-2.44	-2.8	-2.92
9	-1.74	-1.86	-1.98	-2.1	-2.22	-2.34	-2.46	-2.58	-2.7	-2.82	-3.18	-3.3
12	-2.88	-3.0	-3.12	-3.24	-3.36	-3.48	-3.6	-3.72	-3.84	-3.96	-4.32	-4.44
13	-3.26	-3.38	-3.5	-3.62	-3.74	-3.86	-3.98	-4.1	-4.22	-4.34	-4.7	-4.82

Table 8 shows that the highest values for each row are along the first column. The first column encodes the actors that are from the community that were not present in the three days data that were considered for the community labeling. A high value of the similarity warrants a preference for the actors that have the same community membership while a negative alter value favors the actors that have a lower value; similarly the lower membership actors are favored by the negative value of the ego (Table 7). The end result is that for all the row values the actors end up favoring ties with the actor with lowest value of the community membership. This agrees with the intuition as most changes in the network are likely to happen from a actor initiating communication with this new user group.

6   Conclusion and Future Work

In this article, we introduce a general framework for mining social structure from public chat data in virtual worlds and present a comprehensive analysis demonstrating the utility of our techniques for predicting social links and identifying stable communities. The principal contributions of our work are:

1. the creation of an agent architecture suitable for mining social interactions in a variety of massively multi-player online games with minimal modification;
2. introducing two new algorithms for robust conversational partitioning and social network extraction on unstructured dialog data;
3. demonstrating the effectiveness of the conversational partitioning and to/from labeling of our proposed SSTO algorithm;
4. demonstrating the persistence of dialog interaction patterns and communities over time (as mined using our SSTO algorithm) using longitudinal analysis.

Although most earlier studies on group dynamics [30] have been conducted on individuals connected by long-standing social interactions, humans can form groups that exhibit group behavior patterns and biases within a few seconds of minimal interaction, even without face-to-face contact or prior history; Second Life is an interesting research testbed since it contains a large number of groups of this nature. In future work, we plan to do a detailed comparison of the social networks mined from Second Life with those constructed from other sources of data such as blogs, social networking sites, and RSS feeds to better understand the differences between such social networks and those emerging in the virtual world of Second Life.

Acknowledgments. Support for this research was provided by AFOSR YIP award FA9550-09-1-0525 and NSF IIS-08451.

References

1. Adams, P.H., Martell, C.H.: Topic detection and extraction in chat. In: Proceedings of the 2008 IEEE International Conference on Semantic Computing, pp. 581–588. IEEE Computer Society (2008)
2. Bogdanovych, A., Simoff, S., Esteva, M.: Virtual institutions: Normative environments facilitating imitation learning in virtual agents. In: Prendinger, H., Lester, J., Ishizuka, M. (eds.) IVA 2008. LNCS (LNAI), vol. 5208, pp. 456–464. Springer, Heidelberg (2008)
3. Carley, K., Columbus, D., De Reno, M., Bigrigg, M., Diesner, J., Kunkel., F.: AutoMap user's guide. Tech. Rep. CMU-ISR-09-114, Carnegie Mellon University, School of Computer Science, Institute for Software Research (2009)
4. Fisher, D., Turner, T.C., Smith, M.A.: Space planning for online community. In: Proceedings of the Second International Conference on Weblogs and Social Media (2008)
5. Flake, G., Lawrence, S., Giles, C., Coetzee, F.: Self-organization and identification of web communities. Computer 35(3), 66–70 (2002)
6. Forsyth, E., Martell, C.: Lexical and discourse analysis of online chat dialog. In: International Conference on Semantic Computing, pp. 19–26 (2007)
7. Friedman, D., Steed, A., Slater, M.: Spatial social behavior in second life. In: Pelachaud, C., Martin, J.-C., André, E., Chollet, G., Karpouzis, K., Pelé, D. (eds.) IVA 2007. LNCS (LNAI), vol. 4722, pp. 252–263. Springer, Heidelberg (2007)
8. Gerhard, G., Van De Bunt, M.A.V.D., Snijders, T.A.: Friendship networks through time: An actor-oriented dynamic statistical network model. Computational and Mathematical Organization Theory 5(2) (1999)
9. Girvan, M., Newman, M.E.J.: Community structure in social and biological networks. Proceedings of the National Academy of Sciences of the United States of America 99(12), 7821–7826 (2002)
10. Golub, G.H., Loan, C.F.V.: Matrix Computations, 3rd edn. JHU Press (1996)
11. Guimera, R., Amaral, L.A.N.: Functional cartography of complex metabolic networks. Nature 433(7028), 895–900 (2005)
12. Hogg, T., Lerman, K.: Stochastic models of user-contributory web sites. In: Proceedings of the Third International Conference on Weblogs and Social Media (2009)
13. Holme, P., Huss, M., Jeong, H.: Subnetwork hierarchies of biochemical pathways. Bioinformatics 19(4), 532–538 (2003)
14. Huisman, M., Snijders, T.A.B.: Statistical analysis of longitudinal network data with changing composition. Sociological Methods and Research 32, 253–287 (2003)

15. Kahanda, I., Neville, J.: Using transactional information to predict link strength in online so-
    cial networks. In: Proceedings of the Third International Conference on Weblogs and Social
    Media (2009)
16. Lubbers, M.J., Molina, J.L., Lerner, J., Brandes, U., Vila, J., McCarty, C.: Longitudinal anal-
    ysis of personal networks: The case of Argentinean migrants in Spain. Social Networks 32(1),
    91–104 (2010)
17. McGlohon, M., Hurst, M.: Community structure and information flow in Usenet: Improving
    analysis with a thread ownership model. In: Proceedings of the Third International Confer-
    ence on Weblogs and Social Media (2009)
18. Merckena, L., Snijders, T., Steglichd, E., Vartiainene, E., de Vriesa, H.: Dynamics of adoles-
    cent friendship networks and smoking behavior. Social Networks 32, 72–81 (2010)
19. Newman, M.: Finding community structure in networks using the eigenvectors of matrices.
    Phys. Rev. E 74, 036104 (2006)
20. Newman, M.: Modularity and community structure in networks. Proceedings of the National
    Academy of Sciences 103, 8577–8582 (2006)
21. openmetaverse.org: LibOpenMetaverse (2009), http://openmetaverse.org/
    projects/libopenmetaverse (retrieved July 2009)
22. Orkin, J., Roy, D.: The Restaurant Game: Learning social behavior and language from thou-
    sands of players online. Journal of Game Development 3(1), 39–60 (2007)
23. Palla, G., Derenyi, I., Farkas, I., Vicsek, T.: Uncovering the overlapping community structure
    of complex networks in nature and society. Nature 435(7043), 814–818 (2005)
24. Pearson, M., Steglich, C., Snijders, T.: Homophily and assimilation among sport-active ado-
    lescent substance users. Connections 27, 51–67 (2006)
25. Prulj, N.: Biological network comparison using graphlet degree distribution. Bioinformat-
    ics 23(2) (2007)
26. Second Life: Second Life Economic Statistics (2009),
    http://secondlife.com/whatis/economy_stats.php (retrieved July 2009)
27. Shah, F., Sukthankar, G.: Constructing social networks from unstructured group dialog in
    virtual worlds. In: Proceedings of the International Conference on Social Computing and
    Behavioral-Cultural Modeling, College Park, MD, pp. 180–187 (March 2011)
28. Shah, F., Usher, C., Sukthankar, G.: Modeling group dynamics in virtual worlds. In: Proceed-
    ings of the Fourth International Conference on Weblogs and Social Media (2010)
29. Shaikh, S., Strzalkowski, T., Broadwell, A., Stromer-Galley, J., Taylor, S., Webb, N.: Mpc:
    A multi-party chat corpus for modeling social phenomena in discourse. In: Calzolari, N.,
    Choukri, K., Maegaard, B., Mariani, J., Odijk, J., Piperidis, S., Rosner, M., Tapias, D. (eds.)
    Proceedings of the Conference on International Language Resources and Evaluation (LREC
    2010). European Language Resources Association (ELRA) (2010)
30. Shi, L., Huang, W.: Apply social network analysis and data mining to dynamic task synthesis
    to persistent MMORPG virtual world. In: Proceedings of Intelligent Virtual Agents (2004)
31. Snijders, T., van de Bunt, G., Steglich, C.E.G.: Introduction to actor-based models for net-
    work dynamics. Social Networks 32, 44–60 (2010)
32. Snijders, T., Steglich, C.E.G., Schweinberger, M.: Longitudinal models in the behavioral and
    related sciences. Cambridge University Press (2007)
33. Snijders, T.A.B.: Models and methods in social network analysis. Cambridge University
    Press, New York (2005)
34. Snijders, T.A.B.: The statistical evaluation of social network dynamics. Sociological Method-
    ology 31, 361–395 (2001)
35. Snijders, T.A., Ripley, R.M.: Manual for SIENA version 4.0 (2010)
36. Tang, L., Liu, H.: Relational learning via latent social dimensions. In: Proceedings of the
    15th ACM SIGKDD International Conference on Knowledge Discovery and Data Mining,
    pp. 817–826. ACM (2009)

37. Weitnauer, E., Thomas, N.M., Rabe, F., Kopp, S.: Intelligent agents living in social virtual environments – Bringing Max into Second Life. In: Prendinger, H., Lester, J., Ishizuka, M. (eds.) IVA 2008. LNCS (LNAI), vol. 5208, pp. 552–553. Springer, Heidelberg (2008)
38. Wu, T., Khan, F., Fisher, T., Shuler, L., Pottenger, W.: Posting act tagging using transformation based learning. In: The Proceedings of the Workshop on Foundations of Data Mining and Discovery. IEEE International Conference on Data Mining (ICDM) (2002)
39. Zhao, Y., Wang, W.: Attributions of human-avatar relationship closeness in a virtual community. In: Lytras, M.D., Damiani, E., Tennyson, R.D. (eds.) WSKS 2008. LNCS (LNAI), vol. 5288, pp. 61–69. Springer, Heidelberg (2008)

A Multi-agent Architecture to Support Ubiquitous Applications in Smart Environments

Cristiano Maciel[1], Patricia Cristiane de Souza[1], José Viterbo[2],
Fabiana Freitas Mendes[3], and Amal El Fallah Seghrouchni[4]

[1] Instituto de Computação, Universidade Federal de Mato Grosso (UFMT),
Cuiabá, Brazil
{cmaciel,patriciacs}@ufmt.br
[2] Instituto de Computação, Universidade Federal Fluminense (UFF), Niterói, Brazil
viterbo@ic.uff.br
[3] Faculdade UnB Gama, Universidade de Brasília (UnB), Brasília, Brazil
fabianamendes@unb.br
[4] Laboratoire d'Informatique de Paris 6,
Université Pierre et Marie Curie, Paris, France
amal.elfallah@lip6.fr

Abstract. The implementation of Ambient Intelligence (AmI) requires the support of tools and technologies capable of interpreting large quantities of data collected from different sources comprising sensors networks, mobile devices, social networks and other systems. The agent-oriented paradigm is particularly appropriate for such a scenario, because agents offer some important features, like proactive and reactive reasoning, autonomy, social abilities and learning. In this work we propose a middleware architecture to support the development of applications in the scope of Smart Cities, describing its main characteristics and requirements. The Devices, Environments and Social networks Integration Architecture (DESIA) proposal includes emerging technologies such as social networks, cloud computing and digital ecosystems, emphasizing security and privacy, key aspects not always covered by other architectures.

1 Introduction

Citizens with their mobile devices, interacting through social networks and moving around different smart environments such as their homes, offices, schools, universities, hospitals, etc, together with a large number of sensors distributed indoors and outdoors, are the entities that make up a Smart City. Ambient Intelligence (AmI) is a multidisciplinary approach that aims at the integration of innovative sensing, communication and actuation technologies to create computer-mediated environments that support user activities through specific services of the environment, provisioned with minimal user intervention [2], [3]. As such, AmI is the underlying technology necessary to support the integration of the entities that comprise a Smart City: mobile devices, smart environments, social networks and distributed sensors.

The implementation of AmI requires the support of tools and technologies capable of collecting and interpreting large quantities of data collected from

F. Koch et al. (Eds.): CARE/AVSA 2014, CCIS 498, pp. 106–116, 2015.

different sources [11]. The agent-oriented paradigm is particularly appropriate for implementing services to support AmI, because agents offer some features originated from the field of Artificial Intelligence that are vital in such scope: proactive and reactive reasoning, autonomy, social abilities and learning [13]. This paradigm is also useful in modeling real-world and social systems, where optimal solutions are not needed and problems are solved by cooperation and communication, in a fully distributed fashion.

AmI applications must interact with each other in the form of a digital ecosystem of applications and services according to the accepted mobile standards, promoting interoperability and ease of expansion, which makes the development of such applications a very complex task. For this reason, frameworks and middlewares that encapsulate part of this complexity are extremely useful in helping the development of intelligent environments to support smart cities. In this work, we describe the main characteristics and requirements of Devices, Environments and Social networks Integration Architecture (DESIA), an architecture proposal for supporting the development of ubiquitous applications. This architecture is based on two previous works, the Campus Framework [4], [12] and Ao Dai Project [5]. Its primary motivation is to update and expand the main functionalities of those previous works in order to aggregate emerging technologies such as smart cities, sensor networks and social networks, emphasizing security and privacy, aspects not always covered by other architectures.

The present document is organized as follows. Next section provides an overview of the related works. Section 3 presents previous experiences, Section 4 the services, requirements and architecture of the new system, and Section 5 presents the conclusion of this work.

2   Related Work

In a survey concerning context-awareness in ubiquitous media [14], Zhang et al. classify context as physical or virtual based on the context sources. The first one refers to context that can be aggregated by sensing devices (e.g. speed, location, movement, touch) and it is widely used in various context-aware applications. The virtual context is that specified by users or captured from user interactions (e.g, context from reasoning, from applications or from agents). This approach is particularly appropriate, as it deals not only with the physical questions, but also with user preferences, business process, goals and tasks. By investigating the requirements and characteristics of context-awareness, this work proposes a context aware reference framework. The authors classify context-aware in ubiquitous computing into three dimensions: programming abstraction, services and runtime support. Programming abstraction encapsulates and decouples context information to simplify context operations and facilitate the composition and migration of context-aware services. It also defines service interfaces for application developers. Services provide implementation to achieve the abstraction. Runtime support provides an extension to embedded operating systems, for dynamically supporting the self-adaptation of services.

According to Zhang et al. [14], one of the goals of the framework is identifying a set of functionalities and services that simplify the construction of new context-aware applications. This approach is interesting and presents several important elements in this research area. However, according to these authors, it does not discuss context security and privacy that is also a part of runtime support owing to its complexity and dynamics. The use of ubiquitous agents is only mentioned in the study.

Saeed [10], analyzed fifteen context-aware middleware architectures. By examining existing context-aware systems, the author identified some important features for comparison: architectural style, location transparency, aspect-oriented decomposition, fault tolerance, interoperability, service discovery and adaptability. The comparative study discusses several important features, offering an insight into the strengths and weaknesses of each middleware architecture. However, further details of each architecture, such as privacy and the use of agents, may not be assessed by this study.

Martin et al. [8] showed the state of the art of frameworks and middleware systems for supporting the development of mobile and ubiquitous learning applications and provides a comparison of the main functionalities and features of each one selected. Although the study focuses mainly on tools for the development of mobile learning applications, it discusses also several general purpose frameworks.

The frameworks analyzed were classified according to the features indicated by Martin et al. [8]. As key features in the development of context-aware applications in mobile environments, identifies: context acquisition, uncertainty of context data, representation of context data, scalability, synchrony, extensibility and reusability, and privacy.

None of these frameworks approach the privacy problem. The authors believe that this happened because the frameworks analyzed were not yet commercial systems. Nevertheless, great attention should be given to security and privacy, which are fundamental issues to ensure the rights of users.

3   Previous Experiences

The research groups responsible for in this proposal have previously been involved in the development of two frameworks for supporting the implementation of ubiquitous systems, Campus framework and Ao Dai project, which are described as follows.

3.1   Campus Framework

The Campus framework [5] is intended as a configurable framework in which users can decide what services they want to enable in their environments, rather than a monolithic application. It is composed of three levels: the context-provisioning layer, the communication and coordination layer, and the ambient services layer. In a nutshell, the bottom level is responsible for offering basic middleware services and functionality, such as providing context and positioning information and device discovery. Overall communication and coordination is provided by the middle layer that integrates the Campus ontological model to mediation services combined to the coordination protocol [1]. This protocol provides a communication and orchestration layer with software agents in the environment. Finally, the topmost layer provides application specific and ambient services and acts as a hotspot, i.e., allows users to extend the framework by plugging in specific services required by a particular user, environment, type of collaboration, of interest to their environment.

The context-provisioning layer was implemented using the MoCA (Middleware Services for Mobile Collaboration) service-oriented middleware [7,6], which was developed from 2004 to 2009. Although it is a very complex system, it stopped evolving due to changes in the technologies this middleware was related to. MoCA was developed to run in Windows Mobile and Symbian OS. In the course of time, these technologies ran out of use. When MoCA was developed, the idea of mobility was not so spread as it is nowadays. With the popularization of smartphones and tablets, the concept of mobility became extremely important. Therefore, for example, it is no more correct to relate a user of the application to a single device, as a person may have and use more than one device, with different operating systems. Besides, many other technologies were developed disregarding MoCA, such as Bluetooth, 3G and 4G networks and GPS. Thus, the location algorithms must be reviewed to meet new technologies.

3.2   Ao Dai

The Ao Dai project (Agent-Oriented Design for Ambient Intelligence) studies in more detail the connection between agent hierarchy and context-awareness [9]. The challenge in developing a MAS topology that remains decentralized and scalable is how to make the connections between agents related to their context, and how to keep them context-aware when the context changes. The solution is based on two aspects: the use of the agent-oriented, ambient-calculus-inspired programming language CLAIM; and the definition of context-related relations and types of agents.

CLAIM is an agent-oriented programming language that is based on explicit declaration of agent's characteristics: knowledge, goals, messages, and capabilities. All these components are defined using first-order predicate logic and the programmer can program agents by working only at this higher level the Java-based Sympa platform manages the creation, execution and migration of agents.

The idea of the Ao Dai architecture is to map the hierarchy of agents to a hierarchy of contexts, considering physical and computational contexts, as well as user's preferences. Ao Dai use a hierarchical topology, where agents are placed in one or more trees of agents. This is because CLAIM offers the possibility of working easily with agents that are placed in hierarchies, and it is very easy to move whole sub-hierarchies of agents. But Ao Dai consider only two types of context: location and computational resources. These types of context are inherently hierarchical: places are part of larger places, and computational resources cover certain spaces. However, there are also other types of context that are not comprised by Ao Dai, such as social context and users activity [8].

4 Architecture Proposal

In the design of Devices, Environments and Social networks Integration Architecture (DESIA), the Product Overview document follows the structure provided by IEEE Std 1362 (System Definition Concept of Operations). Therefore, this is not a requirement specification. This is a preliminary document generally describing the needs that must be met by the system [6].

4.1 Services

These are the main services to be offered by the system proposed: (1) collection, storage and query of context information; (2) situation inference; (3) user and environment interfaces; and (4) integration with external sources of data. Figure 1 details each service in terms of functionalities and technological standards.

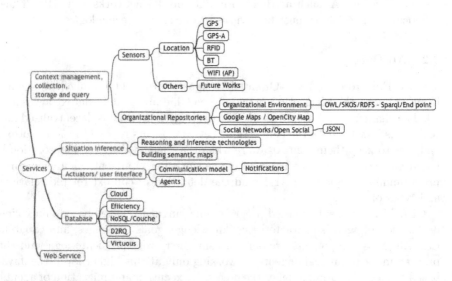

Fig. 1. Services and technological standards of the system

The list of services and their functionalities has been defined under the current technological standards and also taking into account the expertise of the involved researchers. Thus, all requirements necessary to provide the services presented in Figure 1 were collected. A high-level layered representation of the proposed architecture was developed and is discussed in Section 4.3.

4.2 Requirements

The set of requirements that the proposed system must fulfill comprises 31 functional requirements (FR) and 5 non-functional requirements (NFR). These functional requirements were grouped in 7 different categories. The complete list is presented in the Product Overview document [6]. Table 1 summarizes this document, listing the 7 categories and how many functional requirements each of them comprises.

Table 1. Framework functional requirements number

Functional Requirements (FN)	Number of requirements
Location-related requirements (LOC)	4
Context-related requirements (CON)	2
Ecosystems integration (INT)	4
Computational intelligence(SMA)	5
Privacy (PRIV)	5
Security and permissions (SEG)	8
Communication (COM)	3

Among the 31 functional requirements elicited, we selected two in each category to offer the reader an overview on the whole set:

- Location-related requirements
  - LOC-01. The architecture must support location-related definitions in terms of a symbolic space mapping, the meta-classification of all types of environments, the integration of hybrid positioning or composition technologies, distance and route predictions and co-location.
  - LOC-02. Regarding the mapping of symbolic space, the architecture must provide means of physical description in terms of absolute and relative location, physical limits or access limits, and location-related resources.
- Context-related requirements
  - CON-01. The representation of the context must be based on an ontology.
  - CON-02. The following context-related information must be modeled: User profile; Activity (learned activity patterns related either to the environment or to the user); Users roles in the environment; Users status; Technological elements (properties related to the device).
- Requirements related to ecosystems integration
  - INT-01. The architecture must integrate different software and hardware in the same environment.
  - INT-04. The architecture must provide a model for communication and service integration according to the software ecosystems paradigm.
- Requirements related to computational intelligence
  - SMA-02.The architecture must provide support to dynamic inference and notifications (publish/subscribe).

- SMA-03. The architecture must provide support to computational techniques that are appropriate for an intelligent environment model.
  - Privacy-related requirements
    - PRIV-02. The architecture must permit defining information to be protected according to the context and the access levels (religion, sexual orientation, sensitive information, health information etc.)
    - PRIV-03. The architecture must permit defining rules to obtain third parties information, considering confidentiality, reputation mechanisms and information classification, for example.
  - Requirements related to security and permissions
    - SEG-01. The architecture must record the activity log, the places visited and the information accessed.
    - SEG-07. The architecture must provide means to disable/enable availability restrictions, according to institutional rules that were previously defined.

Moreover, the main non-functional requirements (NFR) are presented as follows: [NFR-01] the system must provide all functionalities by means of Wi-Fi, 3G/4G, Bluetooth; [NFR-02] the architecture must provide means for accessibility; [NFR-03] the system developers must use techniques that warrant good usability; [NFR-04] the architecture must consider cultural aspects; [NFR-05] The architecture must provide support to computational techniques that are appropriate for an intelligent environment model by means of artificial neural networks; collective intelligence, artificial immune systems etc.

4.3   DESIA

As depicted in Figure 2, for fulfilling the requirements described in the last section, we propose a multi-agent architecture divided in three different layers, the personal layer, the ambient layer and the cloud layer. The Personal Layer must be implemented in each users personal device. It is responsible for providing the services needed to support the application clients running in such devices and for collecting personal context. This layer is composed by four elements: the Personal Monitoring Agent, the Personal Inference Agent, the Privacy Control Agent and the Personal Context Repository. The Personal Monitoring Agent is responsible for gathering and interpreting context information from the sensors and applications running in the mobile device. The context data will persist in the Personal Context Repository. Part of this context data will be transferred to the cloud, according with the privacy policies established by the user and enforced by the Privacy Control Agent. The Personal Inference Agent is responsible by inferring new context data from the raw context data provided by the Personal Monitoring Agent.

The Ambient Layer must be implemented in each organizational physical environment. It is responsible for providing functionalities to support and integrate the hardware and software entities in such spaces. Similarly, this layer is composed by four elements: the Ambient Monitoring Agent, the Ambient Inference

Agent, the Data Access Control Agent and the Ambient Context Repository. The Ambient Monitoring Agent is responsible for gathering and interpreting context information from the sensors and the several databases distributed in the physical environment or organization. Such data will be persisted in the Ambient Context Repository. While part of this context data may be shared with other organizations and users through the cloud, the Data Access Control Agent Part is responsible applying the organizational policies that define which data must or must not be shared. It manages data of an organization (organization maps, user roles, location of devices, and other resources) and monitors user access, movement and activity in the organization, providing such information to the users and the cloud repositories. The Ambient Inference Agent is responsible by inferring context data from the raw context data provided by the Ambient Monitoring Agent. These agents may be replicated in order to provide scalability.

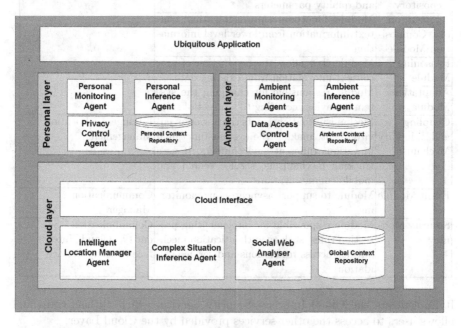

Fig. 2. Devices, Environments and Social networks Integration Architecture (DESIA)

The Cloud Layer is the core of the proposed architecture. It is responsible for integrating data from large groups of users and sets of organizations, gathering social web information, and providing high level inference services. This layer is composed by four elements: the Cloud Interface, the Intelligent Location Manager Agent, the Complex Situation Inference Agent and the Social Web Analyser Agent. The Cloud Interface is responsible for handling all requisitions sent to the services running on the cloud, offering an interface for communication among context repositories in the web, the Intelligent Location Manager Agent and the Complex Situation Inference Agent, which are used by clients applications.

Table 2. Comparative analysis

Element	Description	Architecture Mapping
Sensor	Hardware element responsible for providing context information	Personal and Ambient Layer
Actuator	Hardware element responsible for changing the environment, giving feedback to the user	Ubiquitous Applications
Context Service	Service used to recover context information from sensors. It may aggregate many sensors	Cloud Interface
Actuation Service	Service used to give feedback to the user. It may aggregate many actuators	Access Monitor
Context Repository	Data repository for context information and quality parameters	
Aggregation or Composition Module	Module for composing/aggregating context information from lower level information	
Reasoning Module	Module that allow the production of new context information from existing data	
Adaptation Module	Module responsible for changing the system behavior according to a preset of rules	
Coupling and Mobility Mechanism	Mechanism that abstracts the notion of environment, making the system functional in various different environments. It uses tracking mechanisms, service search and mobile communications	Intelligent Location Management
Event Module	Module to support asynchronous monitoring	Communication Manager
Security Module	Module responsible for implementing protection rules, such as authentication mechanisms, access restrictions and service validation	Communication Security, Cloud Interface Security Service

It implements the Cloud Interface Security Service, which authenticates and allows users to access the other services provided by the Cloud Layer.

The Intelligent Location Manager Agent collects and analyzes location data from users devices. This component is capable of providing location inference based on data collected both from the users devices and from the organizational infrastructures, executing algorithms for analysis and intelligent inference. The Social Web Analyser Agent gathers from the Social Web informations related to the users and organizations. The Complex Situation Inference Agent combines the information provided by those three agents and is capable of executing high level inference, applying machine learning techniques.

Permeating all the three layers we have the Communication Infrastructure, which comprehends the Communication Manager and the Communication Security Service. The Communication Manager manages all clients communications about context information, enforcing privacy policies. The Communication

Security supports security technologies to protect information transfer among different modules of the architecture and devices.

DESIA Analysis. Through a systematic review, we identified architectures for ubiquitous system and common architectural elements for this kind of system. In Table 2, DESIA is compared to the 11 elements of ubiquitous systems we identified. Each of them is presented with a description [7] and the indication of the part of the architecture proposed that implements the element.

From the analysis of Table 2, it is possible to notice that privacy control issues were not discussed in the set of works enumerated in the systematic review, and all items enumerated by [7] are in DESIA. So the main feature implemented by this architecture and the main difference in relation to all others is the concern with privacy issues.

5   Conclusion

This work is result of a research collaboration, which involves members of three universities: Univesidade Federal de Mato Grosso and the Universidade Federal Fluminense, located, respectively, in Cuiab and Niteri, in Brazil, and Universit Pierre et Marie Curie in Paris, France. It aims at specifying Devices, Environments and Social networks Integration Architecture (DESIA), an architecture for supporting the implementation of collaborative applications in the scope of ambient intelligence and smart cities. In DESIA architecture, AmI applications are the basis for the provision of ubiquitous services for citizens in smart cities. New emerging technologies, such as sensor networks, social networks, cloud computing and digital ecosystems, play a fundamental role in the collection, inference and sharing of context information comprising a large number of users distributed in metropolitan-wide areas.

From the study of related work, we identified that security and privacy are fundamental issues. Hence, DESIA provides services to ensure security of personal information. The proposed architecture must manage contracts and rules that govern which kind of information is provided to client applications. This involves the definition of a model for representing types of privacy rules with the use of metrics to evaluate the degree of intrusion and privacy; the elaboration of a set of rules for contract and regulation of multi-agent systems; and the development of a privacy control service.

As ongoing work, we are implementing the Pernonal Layer in Android-based devices. For such purpose, we are adapting SmartAndroid, a platform that implements a framework for developing ubiquitous applications in smart environments. This framework provides context-aware services and supports the implementation of ubiquitous applications, enabling the construction of innovative solutions for residential, trades and industrial environments. Over this platform, sophisticated applications involving resources heterogeneity, context awareness, security and mobility in physical space may be developed. The framework also includes a model of distributed components and event-based communication mechanisms.

References

1. Chourabi, H., Nam, T., Walker, S., Gil-Garcia, J.R., Mellouli, S., Nahon, K., Scholl, H.J.: Understanding smart cities: An integrative framework. In: 45th Hawaii International Conference on System Science (HICSS), pp. 2289–2297 (January 2012)
2. Cook, D.J., Augusto, J.C., Jakkula, V.R.: Ambient intelligence: Technologies, applications, and opportunities. Pervasive and Mobile Computing 5(4), 277–298 (2009)
3. Ducatel, K., Bogdanowicz, M., Scapolo, F., Leijten, J., Burgelman, J.C.: Scenarios for Ambient Intelligence in 2010. Tech. rep., IST Advisory Group (February 2001), ftp://ftp.cordis.lu/pub/ist/docs/istagscenarios2010.pdf
4. El Fallah Seghrouchni, A., Breitman, K., Sabouret, N., Endler, M., Charif, Y., Briot, J.P.: Ambient intelligence applications: Introducing the campus framework. In: 13th IEEE International Conference on Engineering of Complex Computer Systems, ICECCS 2008, pp. 165–174 (March 2008)
5. El Fallah Seghrouchni, A., Olaru, A., Nguyen, N.T.T., Salomone, D.: Ao dai: Agent oriented design for ambient intelligence. In: Desai, N., Liu, A., Winikoff, M. (eds.) PRIMA 2010. LNCS, vol. 7057, pp. 259–269. Springer, Heidelberg (2012)
6. LAVI: Product overview: architecture that supports the development of ubiquitous applica- tions. Tech. rep., Laboratório de Ambientes Virtuais Interativos, Instituto de Computação, Universidade Federal de Mato Grosso, Cuiabá, Brazil (2013)
7. Machado, C., Silva, E., Batista, T., Leite, J., Nakagawa, E.Y.: Architectural elements of ubiquitous systems: A systematic review. In: ICSEA 2013, The Eighth International Conference on Software Engineering Advances, pp. 208–213 (October 2013)
8. Martin, S., Diaz, G., Plaza, I., Ruiz, E., Castro, M., Peire, J.: State of the art of frameworks and middleware for facilitating mobile and ubiquitous learning development. Journal of Systems and Software 84(11), 1883–1891 (2011)
9. O'Grady, M., O'Hare, G.: How smart is your city? Science 335(6076), 1581–1582 (2012)
10. Saeed, A., Waheed, T.: An extensive survey of context-aware middleware architectures. In: 2010 IEEE International Conference on Electro/Information Technology (EIT), pp. 1–6 (May 2010)
11. Viterbo, J., Endler, M.: Decentralized reasoning in ambient intelligence. In: 2009 33rd Annual IEEE on Software Engineering Workshop (SEW), pp. 115–124 (October 2009)
12. Viterbo, J., Mazuel, L., Charif, Y.: Ambient Intelligence: Management of Distributed and Heterogeneous Context Knowledge. In: Context-Aware Computing and Self-Managing Systems, pp. 79–128. CRC/Taylore Francis, Boca Raton (2008)
13. Wooldridge, M.: An Introduction to Multi-Agent Systems. Wiley (2009)
14. Zhang, D., Huang, H., Lai, C.F., Liang, X., Zou, Q., Guo, M.: Survey on context-awareness in ubiquitous media. Multimedia Tools and Applications 1, 1–33 (2011)

Caring for My Neighborhood:
A Platform for Public Oversight

Gisele S. Craveiro and Andrés M.R. Martano

University of São Paulo
Av. Arlindo Béttio, 1000 - 03828-000 - São Paulo - SP - Brazil
{giselesc,andres.martano}@usp.br

Abstract. Social participation is one of the strong claims that have
been done about benefits derived from open government data, but to
achieve this goal there are many social, technical and congnitive barriers to discuss. Regarding the specific example of budget transparency,
despite there is data supply on governments portals, it is not under-
standable yet for a broader audience. In order to address this challenge
we present in this paper Cuidando do Meu Bairro (Caring for My Neighborhood), a tool that was adopted in São Paulo city to promote citizen engagement and better visualization of public budget expenditures.
From unstructured and semi structured information about public spending, some expenditures are geocoded and exhibited on the city map.
The color code used in their pins reflects the real time spending status,
which delivers budgetary content in a more accessible form to the public. We also discuss some challenges faced, the initial users demands and
others ideas to discuss in our ongoing work, the Project Cuidando do
Meu Bairro. A broader picture of this project is presented in order to
give an idea of potential for linking government information about budget actions, budget amendments from the municipal legislative, and the
citizen participation in the budgetary process.

Keywords: geocoding public budget, data visualization, open government data.

1 Introduction

Public budget should express an action plan in order to meet all the needs
and priorities of the people. Its implementation should be as transparent as
possible to allow extensive monitoring by the society. Since 2000, Brazil has been
improving its accountability and transparency with the Fiscal Responsibility
Law [1], amended in 2009 by the Supplemental Law 131 [3], also known as the
Transparency Law. This law states that all Brazilian public entities have to web
publish detailed budget data in a 24-hour basis.

Since 2008 the open data movement introduces new elements related to the
way public data is accessed, used and reused [13]. Open government data (OGD)
refers to releasing freely accessible, standardized and easily readable data. It
promises to make governments more transparent, accountable and efficient. It is

F. Koch et al. (Eds.): CARE/AVSA 2014, CCIS 498, pp. 117–126, 2015.

claimed that it can also foster greater civic participation and promote new business opportunities. Governments, entrepreneurs and civil society organizations all over the world are interested in exploring the potential of open data. As a result, several governments have set up open data portals releasing budget and other public datasets on the Internet.

As the Transparency Law is previous to this, there is no mention about machine readability or other OGD principles [2]. The only guideline closest to them in the legal framework is that all Brazilian public entities must to provide budget data in downloadable datasets, but OGD has been receiving growing attention and some transparency web portals now are compliant to some OGD principles [10]. Government has released hundreds datasets building the basis for several stakeholders to use and re-use information. The idea is to set up collaborative space to partner with civil society and civic entrepreneurs in the development of public services. Individuals and civil society organizations have been developing digital applications in order to generate many points of view regarding these data [9].

Besides the data supply, it is also important to address the point of readability and accessibility of open data, as public information is the foundation of the participatory open data eco-system. But only public information is not enough to create participation, it is key to understand the demand, and the growing importance of this citizenship that is empowered by these data. This can be particularly complex, as we can see in the open budget data case. Open budget data understandability has, at least, two barriers: proficiency in the use of technological tools and knowledge about the public accountancy domain.

Also regarding the demand side for budget data, civil society generally is more focused on the subnational level (cities, districts, counties) budget plan and its execution monitoring. This can be explained by several factors that range from the local and more focused interest (to include and monitor specific projects that benefit a particular community) to a wider scope (national public policies monitoring and evaluation). The scenario of growing decentralization is particularly important in Brazil, where the municipal level plays a fundamental role to deliver health and education public services.

Concerning these motivations we have developed a project named "Cuidando do Meu Bairro"[1] (Caring for My Neighborhood, henceforth CMN). This project aims to provide a tool for citizens to exert social control and oversee individual expenses in the public facilities of their cities. In order to achieve this, São Paulo City's public spendings are geocoded and displayed on a map, allowing anyone interested to follow, in a real time way, individual expenditures. This tool aims to contribute bridging the supply and demand sides.

The remainder of the paper is structured as follows. Related projects are presented and briefly discussed in Section 2. Section 3 presents the tool, its advances, difficulties and other demands. Section 4 addresses our ongoing project and other possible extensions and finally, Section 5 concludes this work.

---

[1] http://cuidando.org.br

2   Related Work

The International Aid Transparency Initiative (IATI) which is a multi-stakeholder initiative that seeks to improve the transparency of aid, developed an XML standard used to share detail on aid projects. The standard is documented[2] and data is available[3]. The standard includes a *Transaction* element[4] which can contain detailed information on financial flows, and also a *Location* element[5] which now makes use of the Mapping for Results geocoding methodology to represent location information. The tools are available in the platform AidData[6]. Development Tracker[7] is another platform that has been developed by UK's Department for International Development (DfID) on top of some IATI files from the government and its partners.

Another important initiative to analyse and visualize public spending is developed by the World Bank in the BOOST program[8]. It seeks to enhance accessibility and use of fiscal data for enhanced expenditure analysis as an input to improved budget processes and outcomes. The geographical tagging is done in a more aggregated level in order to highlight public policies implementation's performance instead of tracking individual projects or activities. The same idea is found in the visualizations delivered by the Open Knowledge's OpenSpending tool[9].

In scientific literature we have found the discussion about budget geocoding in [14]. This paper examines how the display of municipal budget data via web mapping technology allows citizens to visualize how the budget affects their lives and neighborhood. In this study, citizens access Cincinatti's municipal capital budget data via a budget mapping tool. A marker or pin on the map was generated for each capital budget project listed in the database. Markers were color-coded depending on their category. The information provided was not on a real time basis, but the conclusions show that displaying data in map form decreases the barriers citizens go through in order to process and understand budget data. It also increases relevance of the data by showing citizens the effect of the budget in their neighborhood.

3   CMN Tool

The CMN tool essentially collects semi structured public data (XLS files) daily disclosed by the Planning Secretary of São Paulo City's website[10], and places

---

[2] http://iatistandard.org
[3] http://iatiregistry.org
[4] http://iatistandard.org/activities-standard/transaction
[5] http://iatistandard.org/activities-standard/location
[6] http://aiddata.org/maps
[7] http://devtracker.dfid.gov.uk
[8] http://wbi.worldbank.org/boost
[9] https://openspending.org
[10] http://sempla.prefeitura.sp.gov.br/orc_homenew.php

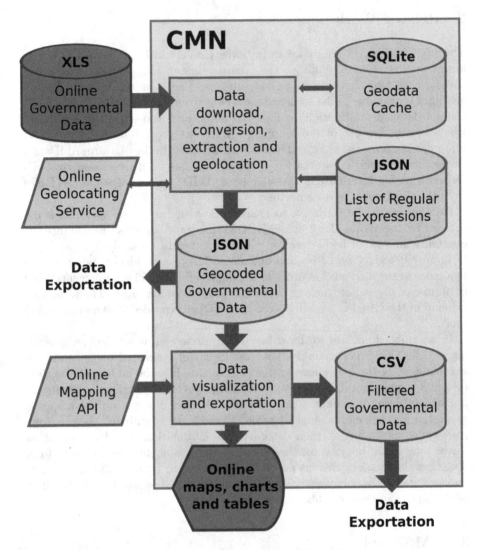

Fig. 1. Architecture of the CMN tool

geographical references on them, generating visualizations for the data, specially a map with different colored pins. Figure 1 describes CMN tool's architecture.

The tool consists mainly of three scripts and a website. The first script, written in Python, downloads the XLS file from the government's website, converts the data to JSON and calls a second Perl script to process the converted data.

This second script applies a list of handmade regular expressions to the data, extracting elements that possibly describe a location, i.e.: "**street** São João" or "**school** Nova Esperança". The same script tries to geolocate these elements

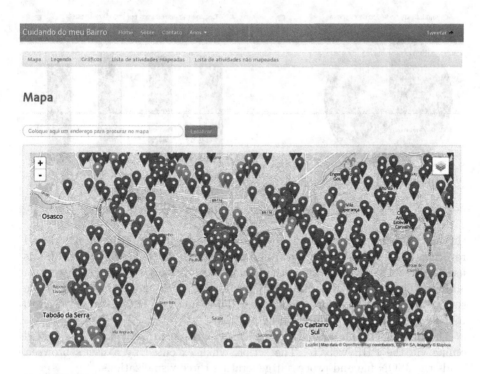

Fig. 2. Public expenditure map from the 2013 Budget in the City of São Paulo, generated by CMN

Fig. 3. Example of one public expenditure detailed information in CMN

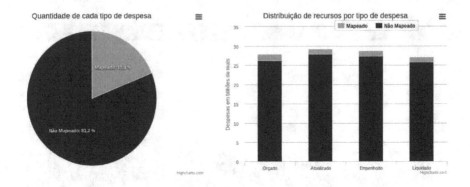

Fig. 4. Charts displaying the percentage of geocoded data

through an online service, saving the whole data (original governmental data and returned latitudes and longitudes) in a final JSON. A local cache, in SQLite, is used to avoid consulting more than once the latitudes and longitudes of an address. This way, if the initial XLS is updated by the government, when the scripts are run again to process the new data, only new addresses will need to be consulted online, speeding up the process.

The final JSON file and the third script, written in JavaScript, are served online via the PHP website. The script, when executed by a user's browser, loads the JSON file and process it generating three visualizations.

The first one is a map with a pin for each geocoded element. Figure 2 shows an example of a public expenditure map from the 2013 Budget in the city of São Paulo generated by the tool. Four colors were used to represent different stages of public expenditure, also exhibited in Figure 2. Budgeted (red color pin) means that it was directly included by a municipal agency or by city councilors amendments. Only after the expense is budgeted, it can receive the *commitment* (green color), which means the reservation of resources after the authorization or signature of service providing contract. Once the commitment is made and the service is performed, the expense is *liquidated* (blue pin). One extra color was included, (yellow color), which shows if there was any change in the budgeted value. It is important to observe that, since the legal framework enforces that all spending data must be updated in a 24-hour basis, CNM tool is configured to extract data from the government's website everyday and refresh the visualizations if needed.

As well as showing the expenditures in the map with their corresponding stages, the following information is presented to detail a specific expense, as shown in the example in Figure 3, and can be displayed by clicking on a pin:

- Identification number;
- Description;
- Budgeted, updated, committed and liquidated values;
- Agency responsible for that expense;
- Agency unit;

- Purpose of the expense, like education or health;
- More specific information on the purpose;

Finally, two charts present the percentage of geocoded data (Figure 4), in numbers of individual expenditures and in amount of money. It is important to display this comparison because there are many expenditures that cannot be placed, or some spending descriptions do not contain any information regarding a location where the money were spent.

The tool was able to identify spendings with a good level of description, however, they have symbolic resources attributed to them and did not progress until the committed or liquidated stages, only staying in the budgeted phase. On the other hand, there are others expenditures with large volumes of resources budgeted, committed and liquidated without any information to help the monitoring of that expense by the citizen. The authors list below the main problems and some examples of spending descriptions in São Paulo city budget:

- Aggregated information: there are projects and activities with large volume of resources that reach the commitment and liquidation phases. However, they do not provide enough details that allows expenditure public oversight. Example: "Operation and Maintenance of Public Libraries", without any detail about which libraries will receive the resource.
- Specific, but only stay in the budgeted stage: these expenditures have detailed description, but they do not progress to the committed stage. Example: "Building of the Municipal Kindergarten School in Vargem Grande neighborhood, in Parelheiros".
- Expenses with symbolic values: a very interesting situation where the tool placed a large number of pins about expenditures with small amount of money planned for them, despite their complexity to implement. These are projects or activities which have approximately 500 USD budget and this is not compatible to the service or good provided, e.g. "Building and Installation of the Municipal Hospital Parelheiros". Also these category of expenses do not reach the commitment phase.

In other to promote reuse of our data, the tool also allows the user to download the final JSON, which has the geocoded data. Besides that, it is also possible to export some filtered data in CSV to the users that want to analyse themselves the public spending divided by agency. In order to promote a wider replication and adoption of this tool, its source code has an open license and is available online[11].

4   CMN Project

This tool is being used by many social leaders and civil society organizations that comprises a network known as "Rede Nossa São Paulo" [12]. It gathers more

---

[11] https://github.com/okfn-brasil/cuidando
[12] http://www.nossasaopaulo.org.br

than 600 civil society organizations working in areas as diverse as education, health, housing, environment, security and leisure.

This project is also a case study in the context of the Open Data Research Network[13], supported by the World Wide Web Foundation and the International Development Research Center (IDRC) and its objective is to give valuable information on how access to budget information affects the relationship between civil society and public administrators in district and municipal levels.

Besides this, we are considering to mine other official sources of information in order to extract details about some expenditures. The main information source is the Official Gazette, which is a PDF document and contains legislation, jurisprudence and administrative actions. It contains a huge amount of information and describes, for instance, bidding and procurement which could substantively improve our project by providing elements for geographic location and other relevant information.

Nevertheless, a large amount of unstructured textual information is supposed to be processed before annotating and validating information that are publicly available. Some definitions found in the literature define semantic annotation as a specific schema to create and use metadata, enabling new methods of access to information [11]. Important related works are OpenCalais [12], Zemanta [4], Ontos [5], TextWise [6], LexML Project [7] and SIOP Project [8].

Another source of information comes from São Paulo City Council, which are the amendments to the city budget. These unstructured information may be parsed and mined in order to build an amendments map, possibly as a layer in CMN website. We also believe that some interesting analysis from 4-years datasets (the period of a city councilman's mandate) may show geographical and political influence in the city. This also may give interesting information about the legislative and executive powers dialogue in order to transform will (amendment) into action (committed and liquidated activities).

The forth and last part comprises support for social interaction. Many alternatives are being considered: interface to social networks, a crowd sourcing platform, and a mobile application. The definitions will rise from discussions, interviews and surveys that are being conducted in the context of our case study in the Open Data Research Network previously presented.

Figure 5 summarizes all the ideas and the ongoing work presented so far.

5   Conclusion

In this paper CMN tool was presented and discussed. With budget geocoding provided, projects are no longer just numbers in a report, but actual improvements or programs down the street from citizens' homes. Comparison between neighborhoods also becomes possible with this mapping tool. More generally, this work presents another way of presenting budgetary information instead of just digitizing existing reports and placing them online, contributing to make data more accessible and relevant to citizens. Basic visualizations, such as graphs,

---

[13] http://opendataresearch.org

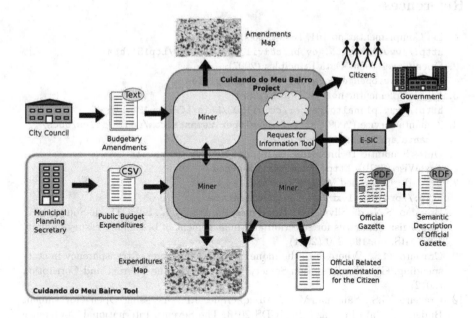

Fig. 5. An overview of CMN Project

provide quick visual comparisons of datasets while maps provide geospatial references. Some related projects presented in this paper provide some or both graphical budgetary visualizations, but this work is the only that shows in a real time basis the city public spending. It makes possible to track the expenditure status, empowering the citizenship and enabling better budget oversight. We also understand that public officials do not have a similar tool and this also could be used to help public administration to be more efficient.

Also a broader scenario of CMN Project was briefly described. Different sources of information, most of them unstructured, are considered in our ongoing work: many of them come from official entities (executive and legislative powers of São Paulo city), but others may come from user interaction (comments, photos, requests for information, etc.). We aim to combine public sector information and crowdsourced data. We hope that this work can show how public information, particularly municipal budgetary data, may influence the relationship between civil society and the government. Moreover, the aim is to bring elements into debate that subside guidelines for building both to civil society and government in order to improve the control mechanisms and monitoring of public resources and help the fight against corruption.

References

1. Lei Complementar no 101, Brasil (2000),
   http://www.planalto.gov.br/ccivil_03/Leis/LCP/Lcp131.htm
2. Open Government Data Principles (2007),
   http://www.opengovdata.org/home/8principles
3. Lei Complementar no 131, Brasil (2009),
   http://www.planalto.gov.br/ccivil_03/Leis/LCP/Lcp131.htm
4. Zemanta service (2009), http://developer.zemanta.com/media/files/docs/
   zemanta_api_companion.pdf
5. Ontos Semantic Technologies (2010), http://www.ontos.com
6. TextWise (2010), http://www.textwise.com
7. LEXML: Controlled Vocabularies (2011),
   http://projeto.lexml.gov.br/documentacao
8. Brandão, S.N., da Silva, T.S., Rodrigues, S., Araujo, L., Silva, D., de Souza, J.M.:
   Siop-legis: Thesaurus for selection and management of brazilian treasury domain.
   In: KMIS, pp. 195–200 (2011)
9. Craveiro, G.S.: Where does the money go? The challenge of transparency in state
   spending. Global Information Society Watch 2012 - The Internet and Corruption
   (2012)
10. Craveiro, G.S., Santana, M.T., Albuquerque, J.P.: Assessing Open Government
    Budgetary Data in Brazil. In: ICDS 2013, The Seventh International Conference
    on Digital Society, pp. 20–27 (2013)
11. Popov, B., Kiryakov, A., Kirilov, A., Manov, D., Ognyanoff, D., Goranov, M.: Kim–
    Semantic annotation platform. In: Fensel, D., Sycara, K., Mylopoulos, J. (eds.)
    ISWC 2003. LNCS, vol. 2870, pp. 834–849. Springer, Heidelberg (2003)
12. Thomas, R.: OpenCalais Documentation (2010),
    http://www.opencalais.com/documentation/opencalais-documentation
13. The 8 Principles of Open Government Data (2007), http://opengovdata.org
14. Walker, S.T.: Budget mapping: Increasing citizen understanding of government
    via interactive design. In: 2014 47th Hawaii International Conference on System
    Sciences, pp. 1–9 (2010)

Author Index